FROGS

IN PHARAOH'S BED

and 49 other fun devotions for kids

D0395354

Mary Rose Pearson

TYNDALE HOUSE PUBLISHERS, INC.
WHEATON, ILLINOIS

To my dear children, Betty Sue, Rose Mary, and David, whose love and devotion to me are only exceeded by their love and devotion to the Lord

CONTENTS

INTRODUCTION

This is a book of facts, Bible stories, and learning activities for children to read and enjoy for themselves, for parents to use in home devotions, or for teachers to employ in any number of church settings. It can be used in home or church schools. Please note, church leaders and teachers, that Tyndale House gives you permission to photocopy the puzzles and quizzes for use in church school, kids groups, etc.

The Bible contains a treasury of exciting adventure stories. Through them, we learn how God worked in the lives of ordinary people like ourselves. They show us the blessings and benefits of trusting and obeying God and the troubles that come from disobeying him. The purpose of this book is to inspire children to love and appreciate God's Book more and to see how it can apply to their own lives.

Learning certain facts can help us understand stories from Bible times better. For this reason, important information is given about objects, places, people, or customs that are a part of the story. The short, interesting facts make the stories come alive and have more meaning. The learning activities are fun and challenging puzzles and quizzes that reinforce the Bible stories and the personal applications.

Many of the Bible stories are ones that are not told as often as some others are. They are not given in chronological order, and each is complete in itself. This means they can be used in the order they're printed or in any order desired.

May our Lord use this book to increase your love for the Grand Old Book that is timeless in meeting the needs of today.

God's Tiny Dive-Bombers

Introduction

"For the Lord your God is the one who goes with you to fight for you against your enemies to give you victory."
(Deuteronomy 20:4)

Zooooom! Ka-pow! A terrific explosion takes place, and an enemy target is destroyed. It is the work of a dive-bomber, a plane that releases its bombs while diving toward a target in enemy territory.

Did you know that God used tiny dive-bombers to help Israel defeat her enemies? He promised to send hornets to drive some of them out. You can read about it in Exodus 23:28.

The Facts, Please!

1. Hornets are a large kind of wasp. They are called "social wasps" because they live in colonies. Each colony has a queen, who lays the eggs. Female workers take care of her by bringing her food and by enlarging the nest to make room for more babies.

2. Wasps are among the most interesting and intelligent insects on earth. They are the world's first papermakers. They take old wood and tough plant fibers, mix them together with saliva, and chew them to a pulp. They flatten this into thin layers of paper, which they use in making their nests.

3. A wasp's nest is made of rows of paper cells, one above the other, like a bee honeycomb. The queen wasp lays her eggs inside these cells. Some hornet nests are as big as a bushel basket!

4. The hornet's stinger, a thin, pointed drill, is found in the rear tip of his abdomen. A sting from a hornet is very painful.

Bible Story: Surprise Attack!
(Deuteronomy 7:1-23)

There it lay, just across the Jordan River—the land of Canaan. At last the Israelites, after 40 years of wandering in the desert, were ready to go in and claim the land God had promised to give them.

Moses had told the people, "When you go into the land, you must destroy the wicked nations that live there, for they hate God and worship idols. Don't be afraid of them. God will deliver them to you and destroy them with a mighty destruction. He will even send hornets among them, so that if any of them hide from you, they will be destroyed."

So the Israelites crossed over the Jordan River. First, God caused the walls of Jericho to fall down flat. Then, in place after place, he helped the Israelites in their battles, as long as they obeyed him and tried to drive out their enemies.

Did God ever send his tiny dive-bombers as he had promised? The Bible doesn't give us the whole story, but it does tell us that God used hornets to help the Israelites. He said to them later, "I sent the hornet ahead of you, which drove your enemies out before you—also the two Amorite kings" (Joshua 24:12).

Let's imagine what that could have been like. Perhaps those kings and their armies were hiding, hoping to make a surprise attack on the Israelites. So God sent in his dive-bombers. *Buzzz! Zap! Buzzz! Zap!* They attacked in huge swarms, stinging every exposed part of the soldiers' bodies. "Help! Let me out of here!" the soldiers must have yelled, waving their arms and slapping at the hornets. They ran out of their hiding places, pursued by the vicious little pests. It was a battle where the Israelites didn't need to use their swords or their bows. Their enemies were driven out by God, who used his tiny dive-bombers—the hornets.

This Is for You

Do we have an enemy? Sure we do, if we're Christians. His name is Satan. His weapons are called "fiery darts" in Ephesians 6:16 (KJV). These are his temptations, by which he tries to get you to sin.

God is more powerful than Satan. He will help us defeat the devil, if we will obey him and use the special weapons he has given us—the Word of God and prayer. Study the Bible and pray for God's help. With God fighting for us, we can zap old Satan's fiery darts every time!

Unscramble Words:
God's Tiny Dive-Bombers

Unscramble the capitalized words to make each statement complete.

1. God's tiny dive-bombers are _____.

    SHNORTE

2. Hornets belong to the family of insects called

    _____.

    PAWSS

3. Hornets are called "social wasps" because they live in

    _____.

    SNOCOLEI

4. Hornets make their paper nests from old _____ and tough _____ _____.   ODOW

    TANPL   SRIBEF

5. A hornet's stinger is located in the rear tip of the

    _____.

    MONDABE

6. The land God gave the Israelites is called _____.

   ANACAN

7. God told the Israelites to drive out or destroy the people who were living in Canaan because they were _____ and _____ _____.

   DICKWE   SHORPWIDE   SLIDO

8. To help drive out Israel's enemies, the Lord sent _____.

   TORNESH

9. A Christian's enemy is _____.

   NATSA

10. Satan's fiery darts are his _____.

    PATTINOSTEM

11. Two weapons you can use against Satan are the _____ and _____.

    LIBBE   YARPRE

12. The one who will give you the most help in your fight against Satan is _____.

    ODG

Dust to Dust

Introduction

"Then shall the dust return to the earth as it was: and the spirit shall return unto God who gave it."

(Ecclesiastes 12:7, KJV)

A boy looked up from his Bible reading and asked his mother, "What does this verse mean: 'Dust thou art, and unto dust shalt thou return'?"

"God made Adam from dust," said his mother. "When Adam died and was buried in the earth, his body became dust again."

"Really?" said the boy. "Hey, then I saw Adam under my bed this morning!"

The Facts, Please!

1. Dust is everywhere—in the air we breathe and on the surface of the things around us. It is on our clothes, our skin, and our hair. It even sits on top of the food we put into our mouths. Did you ever see tiny particles of dust floating in a shaft of sunlight? Then you saw what's in our air all the time.

2. Dust is made up of all kinds of solid matter that is small enough to be carried in the air. Dust particles come from the soil and from bits of mineral matter, soot, volcanic ash, animal and plant tissue, and so on. Parts of you yourself are in the air—millions of your skin cells become dust each day.

3. Dust is constantly traveling. In this very room, there may be dust that was once in China or even in outer space.

4. Many dust particles have been around for years and perhaps for centuries. Actually, flecks of Adam could have been under the boy's bed. Maybe they are in the air you are breathing now!

Bible Story: The Man of Dust
(Genesis 1:26-27; 2:7; 3:19; 1 Corinthians 15:42-44)

It was the sixth day of creation, and God had just made the animals. Our earth had already been created, including its plant life, fish, and birds. Then, after making the animals, God created people, his most important creation of all.

The Bible says God formed man from the dust of the ground—not from the tiny particles of matter that we call dust, but from some of the earth itself. God called the man Adam, which means "out of the ground."

Do you suppose Adam was an apelike creature who could only talk in grunts? That is what some people say the first man was like. But God, who was there, says that he made man in his own likeness. Adam didn't look like God, for God is spirit. But he was like God in his personality. He could reason and talk, he could know right from wrong, and he could love God. God breathed into Adam's body, giving him life. He gave Adam an everlasting soul that could never die.

Adam lived to be 930 years old. Then he died. He was buried in the ground, and after a while, his body became dust. But his soul has lived on for all these thousands of years.

This Is for You

Were we made from a handful of earth? No, but our bodies are made up of some of the same elements as the earth. If we die, our bodies will become part of the dust. The Bible says, "All are of the dust, and all turn to dust again" (Ecclesiastes 3:20, KJV). Our soul, though, will never die. If we are saved, we will go to be with God in heaven. If we have not accepted Jesus as our Savior, we will go to a place of torment.

When Jesus comes again, the bodies of believers who have died will be made alive, all new and perfect (1 Corinthians

15:42-44). The Christians who are still living will have their bodies made new. Then we'll all go to live in heaven forever.

Since dust scatters all over the earth, how can God get a person's body back together again? Well, he made the first man from dust, and he can remake every other person from it, too, can't he? He has the power to bring each body back to life.

Are you saved? Will your body go to heaven when it is resurrected? If not, will you trust Jesus to save you now?

Find the Words:
Angel's Broadcasting System News Bulletin

There is a list of words below the news bulletin. Fill these into the proper blanks to learn some very important news of the future.

It has happened at last! __ __ S __ __ has left

__ __ __ V __ __ and is now in the __ I __ above the

__ __ __ T __. Gabriel's voice was heard, and the

__ __ __ __ P of God sounded. The bodies of __ __ A __

believers that had been __ __ S __ are now __ L __ __ __.

Living believers have their new B __ __ __ __ __. They are

all __ __ __ __ __ __ __ G the L __ __ __ in the air. Soon they

will pass through the __ __ A __ __ __ gates to spend

__ T __ __ __ __ __ __ here. Welcome,

__ H __ __ __ __ __ __ of God! Welcome to the heavenly

__ __ __ Y!

```
──────── Word List ────────
air        dead       Lord
alive      dust       meeting
bodies     earth      pearly
Jesus      eternity   trump
children   heaven     city
```

3

Please Pass the Salt

Introduction

"You are the salt of the earth. But if the salt loses its saltiness, how can it be made salty again? It is no longer good for anything, except to be thrown out and trampled by men."

(Matthew 5:13)

HAS this ever happened to you? You are very hungry. You sit down at the table and thank God for the food. Then you help yourself to the rice, potatoes, or macaroni and take a big bite. Right away you say, *"Ugh!* This doesn't have any taste. Please pass the salt." You add a little salt and taste the food again. Oh, now it's much better!

Those little white grains of salt make a big difference in how our food tastes, don't they? People have been using salt to season their food since very early times. The first mention of it in any writings is found in the Bible. In Job 6:6 the question is asked, "Is tasteless food eaten without salt?"

The Facts, Please!

1. Table salt contains two elements, chlorine and sodium. It is known chemically as sodium chloride.

2. Only a small amount of salt is used for seasoning food. There are about 1,400 other uses.

3. Long ago salt was so important and so scarce that it was used as money. In ancient Greece, slaves were bought with salt. When an owner was pleased with his slave, he said, "He is worth his salt." We still use that phrase to say that someone is worthwhile. In Rome, soldiers received part of their pay in salt. This was called their *salarium,* from which we get our word *salary.*

4. Salt is found in the oceans, in salt lakes, in salt springs, and in salt mines. In the ocean there are about four ounces of salt in every gallon of water. One sea, though, has nine times as much salt as that. The Dead Sea in Israel has 11,600,000,000 tons of salt!

5. In Bible times some of the salt collected from the Dead Sea lost its saltiness. Instead of being thrown away, it was stored in the temple in Jerusalem. It was spread on the marble courtyards when winter rains made them slippery, and people walked on it. That's

what the Bible means when it says salt that has lost
its saltiness is trodden under the feet of men.

6. Long ago, when people signed an agreement, they
ate some salt. It was a pledge of their friendship and
faithfulness.

Bible Story: Yucky Spring Water
(2 Kings 2:20-22)

"What are we going to do?" a man in Jericho asked
his neighbors. "The water flowing from our spring is bad. It
is making us sick, and people are dying."

"Something surely needs to be done," said another man.
"The water is ruining our land, too, and our crops won't
grow."

"I know what we can do," someone spoke up. "The
prophet Elisha has come to live here. He was a follower of
the great prophet Elijah. I have heard that he has power to
do miracles, just like Elijah. Maybe he can help us."

So the men of the city went to Elisha. "This is a beautiful
place to live," they said. "But we can't live here with this
bad water. Could you do anything to help us?"

"Bring me a new bowl filled with salt," said Elisha. With
the bowl in his hand, Elisha went to the spring. He threw
the salt into the water, saying, "The Lord says: 'I have
healed this water. Never again will it cause death or make
the land unproductive.'"

The men tasted the water. It was pure and sweet. From
that time on, the waters were useful. Today the finest spring
in Jericho is called Elisha's Fountain. It is believed to be the

same spring where Elisha threw the salt in and the Lord made the bad waters good.

This Is for You

If we are God's children, Jesus said that we are the salt of the earth. How can that be? First, salt is a preservative. It keeps foods and other items from spoiling and rotting. By our good influence, we can help others not to do sinful things. If we are truly "salty," they will not feel comfortable doing wrong when we are present. Do our friends stop their cursing and dirty jokes when we come around? Do they know that we will not do sinful things or go to bad places with them? Then we are salt that has not lost its saltiness.

Also, salt is used as a seasoning for food. It makes things taste better. By living like Jesus, we can add "flavor" to the world around us. Then other people can "taste and see that the Lord is good" (Psalm 34:8).

A little girl said, "I know what salt does. It makes people thirsty." Are we so "salty" that we make others thirsty to know more about Jesus?

Please Pass the Salt

ACROSS

1 In Jericho, the water from the ____ was bad.
3 Jesus said, "You are the salt of the ____."
6 The people asked ____ to help them.
8 Because of the bad water, the ____ would not grow.
9 The ____ ____ has nine times as much salt as oceans do.

12 Salt is made up of ____ elements.

DOWN
1 Men bought ____ with salt.
2 Elisha performed the miracle because of ____'s power.
4 People got ____ because the water was bad.
5 Long ago, salt was sometimes used as ____.
7 Roman soldiers received salt as part of their ____.
9 The water was so bad that some people even ____.
10 Elisha threw ____ in the spring.
11 Elisha's miracle made the water ____.

The Floating Axhead

Introduction

"Let him have all your worries and cares, for he is always thinking about you and watching everything that concerns you."

(1 Peter 5:7, TLB)

ONE time a little girl whose family was very poor needed shoes. She prayed, "Dear God, please give me a pair of red shoes." Her mother told her that she shouldn't bother God about the color of her shoes. Her daughter replied, "I'll be glad to get any shoes. But I might as well tell God what I'd like best." Soon a package arrived for the little girl with a pair of red shoes inside.

God has a great big universe to run. Does he care about the concerns of a little child? Yes! He knows and cares about what happens to each believer—even the little things. In today's Bible story we'll learn that he cared for the needs of a Bible student who had lost a borrowed tool.

The Facts, Please!

1. Many tools used in Bible times are similar to those we use today (of course, our tools are greatly improved). Various types of saws, axes, hammers, knives, and other tools were common in the ancient world.

2. The first tools were made of stone fastened to wood handles. A very hard stone, flint, was used from earliest times. Copper was the first metal used in tools, but it was too soft. Then bronze, an alloy of copper and tin, was found to be harder and to work better. The Israelites used tools and weapons made from bronze until the days of King Saul.

3. Even before that, the Philistines, Israel's enemies, had learned the secret of how to smelt iron and make tools from it. Iron tools were much harder and sharper than the bronze ones were. When David defeated the Philistines, the Israelites learned their secret of making iron tools and weapons.

4. The ax was an important tool used for felling trees and cutting the logs into lumber. The iron axhead was lashed to a wooden handle by thongs or some other means. This type of fastening often caused an axhead to fly off its handle.

5. Could an iron axhead float on top of water? No, because iron is heavier than water, and the law of gravitation causes it to sink. The only way an iron axhead could float is for God, who created the force of gravity, to temporarily suspend that law.

Bible Story: Axhead, Come to Papa
(2 Kings 6:1-7)

After Elijah was taken up to heaven by a whirlwind, Elisha became the next great prophet. He took over as head teacher of the school of the prophets, where young men learned about God and his laws. They lived together in a dormitory.

One day the young prophets said to Elisha, "There are so many of us in the school that our dormitory has become too small. May we build a new one down in the Jordan River valley? There are plenty of trees there for logs."

"Go," said Elisha.

"Will you go with us, please?" asked a young man.

"I will," answered Elisha.

Soon the sounds of chopping axes rang out in the valley. Suddenly one man's axhead flew off its handle and landed in the river. It sank to the bottom of the swirling, muddy waters and could not be seen. He called out, "Oh, master! It was borrowed."

Elisha knew the young prophet didn't have money to replace the axhead—iron cost a lot of money. "Where did it fall?" he asked. The man pointed to the spot. Elisha cut down a stick and threw it into the water where the man had pointed. Immediately, the axhead came to the surface and floated. God had worked a miracle.

"Grab it," said Elisha. And that's what the young man did.

This Is for You

Elisha threw the stick into the water to show his students a miracle. God made the iron float as though it were a wooden stick. God knew and cared about the need of that young prophet. He suspended the law of gravitation just to help him.

God knows and cares about our small, personal needs. He is very concerned about what happens to us. We don't bother God when we pray about little things. He wants us to talk to him about everything. He is never too busy to hear our prayers. God cared about the little girl who asked for red shoes. He didn't just give her a pair of shoes—he gave her red ones. Does this mean that God gives us everything we ask for? No, not always. He does what is best for us and for his glory. When he says no to one of our prayers, we should thank him for doing what is best.

Give all your cares and worries to Jesus. He cares for you!

Floating Axhead Word Search

Fill in the missing words in the following sentences. Then find those words in the puzzle and circle them. You may go up, down, diagonally, across, or backwards.

1. The little girl asked God for some _____ _____, and he answered her _____.
2. In ancient days, tools were first made from hard _____ and later from _____. Finally, they were made from _____.
3. The prophet who was the head teacher at the school of the _____ was _____.
4. There were so many students living at the school, that they needed more _____.
5. They went to the _____ River to cut down trees and build a bigger place to live.
6. One young man's _____ fell into the _____.
7. He was worried because he had _____ the ax.
8. Elisha threw a _____ into the water, and the axhead _____.
9. _____ worked a miracle by suspending the law of gravitation.

```
V  P  A  I  M  D  A  E  H  X  A
T  R  H  N  A  D  R  O  J  H  D
P  A  S  R  E  B  R  G  G  E  R
R  Y  I  E  N  P  R  C  W  E  G
O  E  L  T  O  P  V  O  D  S  O
P  R  E  A  T  B  R  S  N  S  D
H  E  W  W  S  R  H  B  S  Z  E
E  C  I  Q  O  O  Y  I  T  P  E
T  Q  V  B  E  O  H  R  I  E  T
S  U  K  S  N  M  X  O  C  B  W
F  L  O  A  T  E  D  N  K  L  J
```

The Everlasting Book

Introduction

"The grass withereth, the flower fadeth: but the word of our God shall stand for ever."

(Isaiah 40:8, KJV)

ONCE a Roman emperor ordered that all Bibles should be destroyed. Some Christians planned to hide their Bibles. They pledged to suffer torture or death before they would reveal the hiding places. One day soldiers came to a Christian and demanded to have his Bible. He refused. They beat him badly and threatened to kill him. Finally, he told them where to look. They found a book and burned it.

The Christians asked the man why he gave up his Bible. "I gave them a fake book—not my Bible," he replied.

"Then why did you let them torture you?" he was asked.

"If I had given them the wrong book right away, they would have looked at it carefully and found it was a fake," replied the brave man. "But since I let them torture me, they were sure I had really given them my Bible."

The Facts, Please!

1. The Bible is the most important book ever written. Why? Because God wrote it. He wrote the Ten Commandments with his own fingers on two tablets of stone. The Bible was written over a period of 1,600 years by about 40 men. God told them what to write. "Men spoke from God as they were carried along by the Holy Spirit" (2 Peter 1:21).

2. The majority of the Bible was written on scrolls. These were first made from animal skins, and later from papyrus. It was a material made from the papyrus reed—a plant grown in Egypt. When the original scrolls began to wear out, men called scribes very carefully copied the words onto new scrolls.

   About three hundred years after Christ, books replaced scrolls; but they were still handwritten. In A.D. 1450, when the printing press was invented, the Bible began to be printed much faster.

3. Satan has tried hard to get rid of the Bible. In the past, he has caused wicked men to try to destroy all copies of it. Many, many Christians have given their lives to keep it safe. God will not let his Word be destroyed. "Heaven and earth will pass away, but my words will never pass away" (Matthew 24:35).

Bible Story: God's Book, Slashed and Burned
(Jeremiah 36)

Jehoiakim was a very wicked king who led the Israelites to worship idols and to do other great sins. Jeremiah warned him, "God will punish you and all the people if you keep on sinning."

One day God said to Jeremiah, "Write on a scroll all the words that I have told you about the Israelites and other nations. Maybe they will repent when they hear of the troubles I will bring on them. If they do, I will forgive them."

Jeremiah called for Baruch, his secretary. As Jeremiah dictated God's words, Baruch wrote them on a scroll. After many long hours of work, Jeremiah told Baruch, "I am not allowed to go to the temple now. You go and read the words to the people."

Baruch read from the scroll to a great crowd of people at the temple. Then he read God's words to Judah's officials. When they heard of how God was going to punish them, they were very afraid. "We must tell King Jehoiakim about this," they said.

Jehoiakim listened as a man read the scroll to him. It was wintertime, and he was sitting before an open fire. After hearing some of the scroll, Jehoiakim whipped out a knife, slashed at the scroll, and ripped part of it off. He threw the piece into the fire and watched it burn.

"Stop!" begged three men. "Don't burn the scroll!" Jehoiakim paid no attention. He slashed and burned pieces of the scroll until it was completely destroyed.

"Arrest Jeremiah and Baruch!" ordered the king.

The king's men hunted everywhere, but there was no trace of the two men. How had they disappeared so completely? Where were they? No one knows. It was a perfect hiding place, for God hid them.

This Is for You

The scroll King Jehoiakim destroyed was part of the Word of God. Does that mean that some of God's Word has been lost after all? Oh, no! God told Jeremiah to write all the words again. He dictated every one of them to Baruch another time, and this time God told Jeremiah more words to add to them. We can read these words in our Bible in the book of Jeremiah.

Isn't it wonderful that we can hold the very Word of God in our own hands? Why do you suppose God wrote it? Why has he kept it safe all these years? Why have many people died to keep it from being destroyed? Since God has gone to so much trouble to give the Bible to us, what should we do with it?

God wrote the Bible for us to read. Will you read it every day? He wrote it so that we might believe in Jesus and be saved. Have you done this? He wrote it to tell us what he wants his children to do. Are you obeying what he says?

Match-up:
What Does the Bible Say about Itself?

Look up the verses in your Bible. Draw a line from each sentence to the word in the list that completes it.

1. **Psalm 19:7:** The law of the Lord is   forever

2. **Psalm 12:6:** The words of the Lord   life
   are like purified (refined)

3. **Psalm 119:127:** The psalmist said   perfect
   he loved God's commandments
   more than pure

4. **Deuteronomy 11:27:** If we obey God's   right
   commandments, we will have a

5. **2 Timothy 3:16:** How much Scripture   silver
   is inspired of God (God-breathed)?

6. **Psalm 119:11:** We should hide God's   gold
   Word in our heart that we might not

7. **1 Peter 1:25:** The Word of the Lord lasts   blessing

8. **Psalm 33:4:** The Word of the Lord is   sin

9. **John 20:31:** The Bible was written that   all
   we might believe that Jesus is the Christ,
   the Son of God, and that by believing
   we might have

Strange Little Leather Boxes

Introduction

"Love the Lord your God with all your heart and with all your soul and with all your strength. These commandments that I give you today are to be upon your hearts."

(Deuteronomy 6:5-6)

ONE night about two million slaves escaped from their masters, the Egyptians. God helped them do it. They were his special people, the Israelites. He led them on a long journey over the desert to the land he had given them.

God planned to make these slaves into a great nation that would love and serve him. At Mount Sinai, he gave Moses laws for the people to obey. Moses told the Israelites, "If you will love God with all your heart and obey his laws, he will bless you. Teach these laws to your children. Tie them on your hands and foreheads. Write them on your doorposts." Because of these words, people began to wear some strange little leather boxes.

THE FACTS, PLEASE!

1. The strange little leather boxes were called phylacteries. These boxes were usually 1 1/2 inches square. They were made of the skin of a sheep or cow. Inside the boxes were some of God's laws, written on strips of parchment. These were rolled up and tied with the white hairs of a calf's or a cow's tail. Through a flap in the box, a very long leather strap was passed. Jewish men used the straps to fasten the boxes to their foreheads and to their left arms, near the heart. They wore the boxes during their morning prayers.

2. Why did the men wear the boxes? They thought they were obeying what God said about tying his Word to themselves. There was nothing wrong with doing this, but what God really wanted was for them to love him with all their hearts and to remember his laws and obey them always.

3. When Jesus was on earth, there was a group of religious leaders called Pharisees. They taught God's laws and tried to get people to obey them. Some Pharisees loved and obeyed God. Other Pharisees told people to obey the laws, but they didn't do it themselves. They prayed long prayers on street corners to be seen by men. They wanted people to praise them and call them "master." They wore extra-

large phylacteries to try to show that they were
better than other people.

Bible Story: Good Men and Bad "Good" Men
(Matthew 23:1-8; Luke 18:9-14; John 3; 18:1-11; 19:38-42)

This is a story of two groups of Pharisees. One had
people like Nicodemus and Joseph of Arimathea—they were
good men. The other had people like Simon, Annas, and
Caiaphas. They claimed to be good, but their actions were
bad—they were bad "good" men.

Nicodemus and his friends loved God and tried to obey
his laws. Nicodemus came to see Jesus one night and talked
with him. "You must be born again," Jesus told him. Nicodemus must have believed in Jesus because he helped take
Jesus' body from the cross, and he put expensive spices on
his body in the tomb—a tomb donated by Joseph. Their
hearts were right with God, and their actions proved it.
They were good men.

When the other group of Pharisees prayed in the temple,
they wore extra-large phylacteries on their foreheads and
arms. One prayed, "God, I thank you that I am not like
other men. They are sinful. I fast two times a week, and I
tithe." They prayed loudly on the street corners and made
sure others saw them give money in the temple.

One day Jesus said to a crowd of people, "The Pharisees
tell you many laws to obey, but they don't do these
things themselves. All their works are done to be seen by

men. Their hearts are far from me." This made them very angry.

These Pharisees hated Jesus. They came with the crowd to capture Jesus in the garden. They were at his trial and cried, "Crucify him!" They stood beneath Jesus' cross and made fun of him. They were bad "good" men.

This Is for You

What made the difference in the two groups of Pharisees? It was the condition of their hearts. Nicodemus and Joseph loved God with all their hearts. Jesus was in their hearts. The other Pharisees loved themselves. Their hearts were not right with God. They only claimed to know God.

What is the condition of our heart? Is Jesus there? If he is not there, are we trying to make others think he is? Do we try to talk and act like a Christian? Do we think we're all right because we go to church, give some money to God, and try to be nice to others? If Jesus isn't in our heart, our sins are still there. God sees them, and he won't take us to heaven when we die. Will you let Jesus come into your heart now?

If Jesus is truly our Savior, how much room have we given him in our heart and life? Does he own it all, or have we kept a secret room for ourselves? If you have Jesus in your heart, will you let him now have all of it?

Scrambled Letters:
Professors and Possessors

Finish the six statements by filling in the blanks. Under "Scrambled letters," print the letters as follows: Those with a number 1 underneath go in the first word only; those with a number 2 underneath go in the second word only; those with a number 3 underneath go in both words. Then unscramble the letters to finish the last two sentences.

1. The strange little leather boxes were called
   _ _ _ _ _ _ _ _ _ _ _ _.
      1   3   3

2. These were worn on the arm and on the
   _ _ _ _ _ _ _ _.
      3

3. A very important religious group of Jews was the
   _ _ _ _ _ _ _ _ _ _.
   1 3   2

4. Many Pharisees seemed good, but they didn't love
   _ _ _.
   1

5. One who loved God and came to see Jesus one night
   was named _ _ _ _ _ _ _ _ _ _.
        2   1   2

6. The difference between the good and the bad Pharisees
   was the condition of their _ _ _ _ _ _.
           2   3

Scrambled letters:
   First word: _ _ _ _ _ _ _ _ _ _
   Second word: _ _ _ _ _ _ _ _ _ _

1. A professor of Jesus who doesn't possess him is a
   _ _ _ _ _ _ _ _ _.

2. A possessor of Jesus is a _ _ _ _ _ _ _ _ _ _.

35

The Dagger of the Left-Handed Warrior

Introduction

"Worship the Lord alone. But if you are unwilling to obey the Lord, then decide today whom you will obey. . . . But as for me and my family, we will serve the Lord."

(Joshua 24:14-15, TLB)

HAVE you ever gone through a metal detector in an airport or in some other building? The detector buzzes when metal passes through it. Often detectors are set off by harmless metal objects, but their purpose is to locate dangerous weapons when someone tries to smuggle them on board a plane or inside a building.

Our story is about a Bible hero who entered a king's house

with a weapon that would have set off a metal detector, if it had been invented then. His weapon was a dagger.

The Facts, Please!

1. A dagger is a weapon with a sharp point, like a sword, but shorter. Its two parts are a blade with a double edge, from six to eighteen inches long, and a hilt (handle).

2. Swords and daggers were the basic weapons for offensive warfare in Bible times and were used to cut and stab. They were usually worn in a sheath, attached to the left side of a man's belt, so he could grab his weapon with his right hand.

3. When the Israelites entered Canaan, they immediately had war. The people already living there worshiped idols and even sacrificed their children on idol altars. God told the Israelites to drive out all the Canaanites. If they didn't, they would be tempted to worship idols instead of the true God.

4. The Israelites fought battles and drove out or killed many of the wicked people—but not all of them. After a while the men of Israel began to marry the women of Canaan and to bow before their false gods, just as God had said. Because of this, God allowed other nations to attack and conquer them.

5. God's people were very miserable. Finally, they turned from idol worship and cried to God, "Send someone to deliver us from our enemies." Over and

over, for about three hundred years, they worshiped idols, got in trouble, and then called on God. Each time he sent a brave hero or heroine to free them.

Bible Story: A Fat King Gets the Dagger
(Judges 3:12-30)

The Israelites were doing it again—bowing to Baal, a false god, and forgetting about the true God. In Moab, a nearby country, lived a very fat king named Eglon. "Those Israelites are getting rich with their fields and flocks of animals," he told his soldiers. "Let's conquer them and make them pay us money." God allowed King Eglon to do it. For eighteen years, Eglon lived at Jericho and ruled the Israelites. They became poor and unhappy. They cried for God to save them, and he helped Ehud set them free. This is how he did it.

One day Ehud went with some other men to take the tribute money to the king. Before going, Ehud made himself a dagger. Because he was left-handed, he strapped it to his right thigh, hiding it under his clothing. At the king's house, guards examined Ehud and his men for weapons, looking only on the left side. They found none. The men gave their money to the king and started for home.

Soon Ehud turned back to the king's house. Passing freely past the guards, he came into Eglon's room. "I have a secret message for you," he said. The king dismissed his servants, and Ehud said, "My message is from God."

As Eglon stood up, Ehud drew his dagger and plunged it

into the king's huge, flabby stomach. Then he left the room, locking the door behind him. The servants waited for the king to call them, but he never did. Finally, they got a key and opened the door. There, on the floor, lay their dead king.

Ehud hurried back to his mountain home. Placing a trumpet to his lips, he blew a long, loud blast. Men who lived on the surrounding mountains heard it and ran to Ehud, carrying their weapons. "Follow me," he said, "for the Lord has given the men of Moab into your hands." That day the Israelites killed 10,000 Moabites, and God gave them peace for 80 years.

This Is for You

Ehud lived at a time when very few people loved and served the true God. He had to choose if he would be like them or serve the Lord. He chose to be on God's side. This meant he had to go on a very dangerous mission. When he did, God took care of him, and Israel had peace for a long time.

Have we ever felt that we were the only one among our schoolmates who loved God and wanted to do right? Is it hard to find any Christian friends in our neighborhood? Perhaps we are the only member of our family who is a Christian. What should we do—stand up and be counted on God's side or just keep quiet and go along with the crowd? It's a tough decision sometimes. But there's only one right thing to do: Choose to follow the Lord. We'll always be glad we did.

Letter Maze:
Who Is on the Lord's Side?

After the Israelites worshiped a golden calf, Moses asked, "Who is on the Lord's side?" (Exodus 32:26, KJV). His words are repeated three times in this maze. Go through it, picking up the letters of these words in their correct order. You may go up, down, right, and left. Then sign your name in the bottom corner if you are on the Lord's side.

H	W	O	N	E	L	O	R
O	I	S	T	H	D	I	D
O	S	I	W	?	E	S	S
N	T	O	H	E	?	W	H
E	H	D	S	D	H	T	O
L	O	R	S	I	E	N	I
D	I	S	R	O	L	O	S
E	?	S	D				

A Rainbow's "Pot of Gold"

Introduction

"Praise be to the Lord. . . . Not one word has failed of all the good promises he gave."

(1 Kings 8:56)

WHILE World War II raged in Europe, 120 missionaries and their children sailed from New York for Africa one day aboard a neutral ship, the *Zamzam*. After many days at sea, their ship was bombed by a German raider ship. The passengers abandoned their ship and climbed into lifeboats or floated in the sea.

Later they were picked up by the same German raider that had destroyed their ship. The shivering, dripping-wet survivors stood on its deck and looked at the badly listing *Zamzam*. They didn't know what would happen to them or how they would be treated. But then, in a clear sky, a rainbow appeared. To the missionaries, it was God's promise that he would take care of them. "Safe am I, in the hollow of his hand," they sang.

They had many frightening experiences during a month at sea and a month on land in German territory. Then God helped all of them to return safely to America. He had kept his promise.

The Facts, Please!

1. A rainbow is an arch of beautiful colors that may appear in the sky after a rainstorm. We can only see it when the sun is behind us and rain or a mist is in front of us. Sometimes the bow may spread all the way across the sky, with its two ends seeming to touch the earth.

2. There are seven colors in each bow—violet, indigo, blue, green, yellow, orange, and red. The red is at the top of the arch. The colors blend into one another so that we rarely see more than four or five of them clearly.

3. Rainbows are caused by sunlight striking drops of water. The sunlight hits the falling raindrops, which then act as prisms, reflecting the light. The different colors are formed as the light passes through the raindrops at the different angles.

4. A rainbow is actually a full circle. When the sun is near the horizon, a person on a high mountain or in a plane might see the complete circle.

5. Sometimes there may be a primary and a secondary rainbow, whose colors are in reverse and less brilliant. The moon can also have a rainbow in softer colors.

6. An old legend says that there is a pot of gold at the end of the rainbow, and whoever finds it can keep it. Once a man set out to find the pot of gold, but it always seemed to be just beyond him. Of course, he never found it.

Bible Story: The Promise in the Sky
(Genesis 7:1–9:17)

Noah and his family—and all the animals—had boarded the ark when the sky suddenly became black with clouds. The earth trembled and shook, and subterranean waters burst forth from the earth. Great torrents of rain poured from the sky. For forty days and nights the flooding continued, until the whole earth was one great ocean—not even the mountaintops showed.

On top of the water floated the huge, strange-looking boat that Noah had built according to God's directions. After five months the flood waters began to go down, and the boat finally settled on a mountain. Later, after the people and animals had been on board the ark for a little more than a year, God told them they could leave it.

When at last they stepped out of the ark, what a different and strange world they saw! The face of the earth must have been far different from what it had been before. There were no buildings left standing, and all people and animals were dead.

The very first thing Noah did was to build an altar and sacrifice animals and birds on it. He thanked God for taking care of them in the awful flood. God told Noah, "I have placed my rainbow in the clouds as a promise that I will never again kill all living things. I will never send another flood to destroy the earth."

After that, every time he saw a rainbow, Noah must have been very happy, for he knew that God always keeps his promises.

This Is for You

"I promise!" someone says to us. Can we count on those words? Sometimes we can, and sometimes we can't. The statement is easy to say but hard to keep. This is not true of God. When he says something, it is as good as done. He never breaks a promise.

The rainbow was a sign in the sky that God would never destroy all living things by a flood again. He has kept that promise. When we look at a rainbow, we can remember this and be thankful. We can also remember that God keeps all his promises. God must have worked a miracle for the missionaries to see a rainbow in a clear sky. They saw it and knew God would take care of them. And he did!

Yes, there is a pot of gold in a rainbow—not something we can touch, but a sure knowledge that God will keep all the promises he has given us in his Word. Whenever we need his help, we know that God does what he says he will do. We can count on it. That's better than having all the gold in the world.

How to Claim God's Promises

Not all promises in the Bible are for everyone. There are special promises that God made to the Jews in Bible times, and some are for the future. Many promises are for God's children today. Each comes with a condition—something we must do before God will fulfill the promise.

Look up each reference given in the puzzle and draw a line from it to the words that tell what God promises in the verse. Then draw a line from the reference to what you must do to claim the promise. The first one is done for you.

Cleansing from sin	Psalm 119:165	Obey and please God
Long life	1 John 3:22	Love God's laws
Gifts from God	Ephesians 6:2-3	Confess sins
Wisdom	1 John 1:9	Have clean hands and a pure heart
Answers to prayer	Luke 6:38	Ask and believe God
Blessings from God	James 1:5-6	Honor your parents
Peace	Psalm 24:4-5	Give to God

Is the Yoke on You?

Introduction

"Take my yoke upon you, and learn of me; for I am meek and lowly in heart: and ye shall find rest unto your souls. For my yoke is easy, and my burden is light."
(Matthew 11:29-30, KJV)

TWO Americans visiting in Korea saw a boy pulling a plow while an old man tried to guide it. The Americans were amused and took a picture of the scene. "They must be very poor," one said to the missionary who was with them.

"Yes, they are," said the missionary. "When the church was being built, they were eager to give something. They had no money, so they sold their ox and gave the money from the sale to the church. Now they pull the plow themselves."

"What a great sacrifice!" exclaimed one American.

"They didn't call it a sacrifice," said the missionary. "They felt it was fortunate they had the ox to sell."

The Facts, Please!

Facts about two items are important for this Bible story.

A Yoke

1. In Bible times, a yoke was a rough wooden beam shaped to fit across the necks of a pair of animals. It was held in place by two sticks that came down the sides of the necks and were held together by ropes or leather fasteners.

2. Oxen were the animals usually used in working the land or pulling loads. A yoke linked the oxen together so they could work more efficiently.

3. In Jesus' day, the Jewish rabbis (teachers) used the phrase "take the yoke of" to mean "become the pupil of" a certain teacher.

A Mantle

1. A mantle (a coat or cloak) was an almost square piece of cloth, worn on top of other clothing. It was usually made of two pieces of thick woolen material sewn together, with slits for the arms. A prophet's mantle was, as a rule, a sheepskin with the wool turned outward. This is probably the kind of mantle worn by the prophet Elijah.

2. If a prophet wished to appoint a man to be prophet in his place after he was gone, he would throw his mantle over the man's shoulders. This meant that he was the man best suited to do the job.

Bible Story: A Yoke of Oxen, a Mantle, and the Yoke of God
(1 Kings 19:15-21)

In the beautiful hill country near the Jordan River lived a young man named Elisha. He was the son of a rich farmer. At that time, most of the Israelites worshiped Baal, a false god. Elisha was one of only seven thousand Israelites who worshiped the true God.

One day God said to the prophet Elijah, "Find Elisha and anoint him to take your place as my prophet." Elijah began a long journey through the wilderness and the lands of Judah and Israel. At last he came to the farm of Elisha's father.

Elisha was plowing in a field with a pair of oxen. Eleven other teams of oxen plowed ahead of him. Elisha saw a rough, strange-looking man walking toward him. He was wearing a sheepskin mantle. Why, that was the great prophet Elijah!

Elijah walked up to Elisha without saying a word. He threw his mantle over the young man's shoulders and walked on. Elisha knew he had been chosen to leave his comfortable home and follow Elijah in the life of a prophet. He would be hated by the queen and other Baal worshipers. Perhaps he'd even be killed.

Elisha stopped his plowing and ran after Elijah. "Let me kiss my parents good-bye first," he said. Elijah agreed.

After he said his good-byes to his parents, Elisha killed his pair of oxen. He built a fire with the yoke and wooden plow and roasted the meat. He had a great feast for all the farm workers. Then, leaving his home behind, he walked away to serve God alongside Elijah.

This Is for You

Jesus said, "Take my yoke upon you, and learn of me." The people who heard him speak knew what he meant. He wanted them to become his followers and let him teach them. Jesus said he had a yoke. What was his yoke? It was that he came to do his Father's will. For him, it meant going to the cross and dying for our sins. If we take his yoke upon us, we will say, "Heavenly Father, I will do whatever you want me to do."

Elisha exchanged his yoke of oxen for the yoke of God. He became a great miracle worker and servant of the Lord. The poor Korean father and son took an actual yoke upon themselves and plowed their fields in order to put on God's yoke and serve him.

Is God's yoke on you? Have you received Jesus as Savior? Have you given your life to him? Do you think it's too hard to follow Jesus? It isn't. He said, "My yoke is easy, and my burden is light." Jesus gives us such joy and peace inside when we take his yoke that nothing else in life can be so good.

Yokes and Mantles

ACROSS

4 To "take the yoke of" means to follow a certain _____.
5 _____ were commonly used for pulling a plow.
10 A yoke was usually made from _____.
11 A man's coat worn over his other clothes was called a _____.
12 Elisha lived near the _____ River.

DOWN

1 Only 7,000 Israelites did not worship the false god _____.
2 A prophet's mantle was made of _____.
3 Elijah was a great _____.

6 God chose _____ to be the prophet after Elijah.
7 Elisha was the son of a rich _____.
8 A harness that connected a pair of animals for work was called a _____.
9 _____ put his mantle on Elisha's shoulders.

10

The Wise Potter and the Lump of Clay

Introduction

"Shall what is formed say to him who formed it, 'Why did you make me like this?' Does not the potter have the right to make out of the same lump of clay some pottery for noble purposes and some for common use?"

(Romans 9:20-21)

HAVE you ever made things from modeling clay? Was each piece perfect the first time? Probably not. But you could smash it flat and remake it, couldn't you? Let's imagine what that must be like for a lump of clay. You mold it into a shape, but it's not what you want. You smash it into a shapeless mass again. "Ouch!" says the clay. "That hurts. Don't smash me like that. And don't make me into a cat. I want to be a dog."

Foolish clay. It doesn't have the right to tell you what to do with it. It's your clay. You can smash it and mold it into whatever shape you'd like.

The Facts, Please!

1. People who work with clay are called potters. The making of pottery is one of the earliest crafts of civilization. One of man's first inventions was the potter's wheel.

2. The clay used in pottery has two characteristics: It can be shaped (and retain its shape), and it hardens under a high temperature. In Bible times, clay was mixed with water and sifted to remove stones and other impurities. Then it was trampled until it was smooth and pliable. At the potter's bench, more water was added until it was just right for molding.

3. The earliest potter's wheel consisted of a horizontal turntable made from wood, clay, or limestone. It was turned by hand on an axle that pierced the workbench. One person turned the wheel, while another one shaped the clay. This was the kind of wheel Jeremiah saw when he went to the potter's house.

    About 200 B.C., a better wheel was invented, consisting of a larger second wheel on the bottom end of the axle. A potter could turn it with his feet and make the upper wheel turn as he molded the clay.

4. Sometimes air bubbles developed in the pottery, or it didn't come out just right. Then the potter would smash the clay flat and begin again.

5. After molding, pottery was air-dried and then hardened in a kiln that was fired to a very high temperature.

Bible Story: The Potter and the Smashed Pot
(Jeremiah 18:1-10)

The Lord spoke to the prophet Jeremiah one day: "Go down to the potter's house, and I will tell you something there."

Jeremiah went at once. At the potter's house he saw molded pots, jars, and bowls drying in the air. There was a big heap of clay on the floor beside a potter's wheel.

The potter trampled the heap of clay with his feet, smashing and stomping it until it was smooth. He picked up a lump, added a little water, and kneaded it with his hands. Then he threw the lump on the center of the wheel.

As an assistant turned the wheel, the potter drew the revolving clay up with his thumbs and fingers to the desired shape. "Stop the wheel," he said suddenly. "This isn't coming out right." The potter smashed the clay until it was just a lump again. He kneaded it smooth and then molded it on the wheel all over again. This time he made a beautiful pot.

Jeremiah heard the Lord speak again: "O Israel, can't I do to you as this potter has done to the clay? As the clay is in the potter's hands, so you are in my hands. I can make a nation, and I can destroy it if the people become evil. If they repent of evil, I will not destroy them. If they will not obey me, I will not bless them."

Jeremiah told God's words to the people, but they said, "Don't bother telling us. We will do what we want to do."

This Is for You

Does God have a right to tell us what to do? Yes, he has every right. He made us. He is the Potter, and we are the clay. He wants to keep on working with us to make us the best that we can be. He puts us on his wheel and molds us through the things that happen in our life. He has a special plan for our life and jobs he wants us to do. He wants us to be faithful Christians.

What if we don't always follow God's plan? What if we try to do things our own way? Then we are like the clay that gets marred as the potter is molding it. What then? God doesn't throw us away. He allows things to happen in our life to turn us back to him. He "smashes" us and begins to mold us again. When troubles come to us, is God always punishing us for being bad? Not always. Sometimes he allows these events to bring out the best in us and to make us more like himself. We shouldn't get mad at God for doing that. Instead, we should be like the pliable clay and let the Potter do his work. He knows what is best.

What Does God Want You to Do?

Print letters in the blanks to form the words that are missing in the sentences. Then place the letters with numbers below them in the blanks with the same number at the end of this puzzle.

1. Workers with clay are called __ __ __ __ __ __ __.
                                   3

2. They can only work with a special kind of __ __ __ __.
             7   10,11

3. Pottery clay must be able to retain its __ __ __ __ __.
                               1

4. It must harden under a high __ __ __ __ __ __ __ __ __
                       4

   __ __.
   13

5. Pottery is molded on a potter's __ __ __ __ __.
                       5   14

6. The man God sent to the potter's house was __ __ __ __
                       6

   __ __ __ __.
   12

7. The potter had a marred pot that he __ __ __ __ __ __ __
                       9

   and __ __ __ __ __ __.
      2 8

God is our __ __ __ __ __ __.
        1 2 3 4 5 6

We are his __ __ __ __.
        7 8 9 10

He wants us to __ __ __ __ __ ourselves to him.
          11 12 13 14 15

11

The Strange Time of the Sundial

Introduction

"O Lord God! You have made the heavens and earth by your great power; nothing is too hard for you!"
(Jeremiah 32:17, TLB)

Do you have a watch? Does your watch tell time? Probably not. Most watches don't tell time—they can't talk. Seriously, do you know what time it is? If you don't know, you can look at a clock or watch and find out, can't you? Most likely you can find out not only the hour and the minute but even the second.

If you had lived in Bible times, you couldn't have been so exact. The only way to tell time was on a sundial.

The Facts, Please!

1. Ancient people did not measure time by hours and minutes or even by days. They were most concerned with seasons of the year in order to know when to plant their crops. They judged the seasons by the constellations of stars, which appeared in different parts of the sky in different seasons.

2. The oldest device for measuring hours of the day is the sundial. It is based on the fact that the shadow of an object will move from one side of the object to the other as the sun moves from east to west during the day.

3. The most common kind of sundial is made up of two parts—the dial face and the pointer, called the gnomon. The round dial face is horizontal and divided into quarters by lines running toward the four points of the compass. These are further divided into hours and sometimes half or quarter hours. The pointer is a metal triangle, placed in the center of the dial and pointing toward the North Pole. As the sun moves across the horizon, the shadow of a sundial's pointer moves across the dial face.

4. In the story of King Hezekiah, he had a sundial in his courtyard called "the dial (or steps) of Ahaz." This may have been a stairway going up the sides of an obelisk, with its point serving as a pointer. Its shadow would be on the highest step at high noon and in the morning and evening on the lowest steps

on one side or another. The steps may have measured time at the rate of a half hour per step.

Bible Story: When the Sun's Shadow Moved Backward
(2 Kings 20:1-21; Isaiah 38:1-8)

King Hezekiah was a good king who trusted in the Lord and kept his commandments. One day he became very sick. The prophet Isaiah came to him with a message. "God says that you must take care of all your affairs, for you are going to die."

What terrible news! Hezekiah was only 39 years old. He hadn't done all the work he wanted to do as king. Also, he didn't yet have a son to be king in his place. He turned his face to the wall to pray. "O Lord," he pleaded, "remember that I have tried to obey you in all things!" Then he broke down and cried.

Isaiah left the king's bedroom and walked out into the courtyard, but there God stopped him. "Go back and tell Hezekiah these words from me, 'I have heard your prayer and seen your tears. I will heal you. Three days from now you will go into the temple. I will add to your life 15 years, and I will deliver your city from its enemies, the Assyrians.'"

"How can I know all of this will happen?" the king asked Isaiah. "Do a miracle to prove it is true."

"Do you want the shadow on the sundial to go forward 10 steps or backward 10 steps?" asked Isaiah.

"Backward 10 steps," said Hezekiah. "That would be much harder to do."

Isaiah asked the Lord to work the miracle, and the shadow moved back 10 steps on the sundial of Ahaz.

God did just what he had promised. Hezekiah lived 15 more years, and his city was delivered from the Assyrians. God gave him a son, who was 12 years old when Hezekiah died.

This Is for You

How did God cause the sundial to go backward? The Bible doesn't tell us. But it says it happened, so we know it did. God created the world and set its laws in motion. When he wants to, he can change the laws of nature. He worked a miracle—an act of God that changes the natural order of things. It is something that no man can do.

God has all power. He can do anything he wants to do. Nothing is too hard for him. What does that mean for us? It means he has the ability to answer our prayers. We can pray to him about everything in our life—the little things as well as the big.

Coded Message:
What Is the Most Important Time?

Isaiah told King Hezekiah that his time had just about run out. Hezekiah prayed, and God gave him fifteen more years of life. He knew then how much time he had left in his life. But we don't know how long we will live. Jesus may come back at any time. We must trust Jesus to save us before anything happens to us or before Jesus returns. So when is the most important time to ask Jesus to save you? Using the code below, fill in the letters above the clock hours in the Bible verse quote. This will give you the answer.

Letters: I S H N A T E O D P L W

Hours: 1 2 3 4 5 6 7 8 9 10 11 12

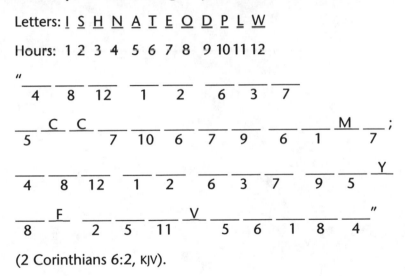

```
"  ___  ___  ___   ___  ___   ___  ___  ___
    4    8   12    1    2     6    3    7

___   C   C   ___  ___  ___  ___  ___  ___   M  ___ ;
 5            7   10    6    7    9    6    1       7

___  ___  ___   ___  ___   ___  ___  ___   ___  ___  Y
 4    8   12    1    2     6    3    7     9    5

___   F   ___  ___   V   ___  ___  ___  ___  ___ "
 8    2    5   11    5    6    1    8    4
```

(2 Corinthians 6:2, KJV).

12

Giant Mountain Men

Introduction

"Be strong and of a good courage; be not afraid, neither be thou dismayed: for the Lord thy God is with thee whithersoever thou goest."

(Joshua 1:9, KJV)

When you were little, did you enjoy hearing stories about giants? In the story "Jack and the Beanstalk," were you frightened when the giant roared, "Fe-fi-fo-fum! I smell the blood of an Englishman"? A story like that is scary for little kids; but when you're older, you know it's only a fairy tale.

Are you thrilled with the true story of David and Goliath? Do you admire the courage of David, who was too young to be a soldier but was braver than any man in Israel's army?

Goliath is the best-known giant, but the Bible tells of other giants, also.

The Facts, Please!

1. A giant human being is one who is very much larger than normal. Some giants may be taller than nine feet.

2. Many people grow extra tall naturally (like a seven-foot basketball star, for instance). A real giant has a condition known as gigantism or giantism. It begins in childhood and is caused when the growth hormones in the pituitary gland are overactive. Today there are treatments for this condition.

3. Giants are mentioned in the Bible in several places. There were giants in the land in Noah's day. A great many giants lived in a valley in Canaan when Abraham lived there. The last of these valley giants was Og, king of Bashan. He had an iron bed that was 13 feet long and 6 feet wide. Later, when the Israelites came to the border of Canaan, they were afraid to go into their land because of the giants there. King David's soldiers killed four giants. One of them had six fingers on each hand and six toes on each foot.

4. Giants were not only huge in size, they had great strength. That's why ordinary-size men were afraid to fight them. Those who did go against them—like young David—trusted God to help them. They knew God is more powerful than any giant.

Bible Story: A "Grasshopper" Defeats the Giants
(Numbers 13; Joshua 14:6-15; 15:13-15)

An old man, Caleb, stood looking at a mountain and the land surrounding it. "This is the land Moses gave me and my family for our inheritance," he told his relatives. "Forty-five years ago I walked across this very place when I was one of the 12 spies. Now let's go to Joshua and claim our land."

Caleb said to Joshua, "You and I were among the 12 men who spied out the land of Canaan. Ten spies made the people afraid to go in and take the land God had given us. They said, 'It is a wonderful land, flowing with milk and honey. But the cities are well fortified. We saw giants there. Compared to them, we were like grasshoppers! We can't fight them.'

"I said, 'Let's go up at once. We are well able to take the land!' And you agreed with me. But the Israelites would not trust God and go. So we wandered in the wilderness for 40 years until all those adults were dead, except you and me.

"When we finally came into Canaan, I helped you drive out many of the wicked people. Now you are dividing the land. I want this mountain, where we walked as spies. I know some giants still live there; and there are great, walled cities.

"I am 85 years old, but I am as strong as ever. With the Lord's help, I will drive out the giants." Joshua gave him the land. Brave Caleb, with his men, fought the tall and mighty giants and drove them out. Then they moved onto their land. And that's how the "grasshopper" defeated the giants.

This Is for You

God told the Israelites to go into Canaan and claim their land by driving out the wicked people there— even the giants. Most of them were afraid to obey God. Compared to the giants, they felt like grasshoppers. Only Caleb and Joshua were not afraid.

Are there some things we know God wants us to do? Are we afraid of doing some of them? Perhaps it's telling our schoolmates or family about Jesus. Maybe it's saying no to sinful things we're asked to do. Or it could be singing a special number in church or speaking in our Sunday school class. Doing God's will is like climbing a mountain where the "giants" of fear or discouragement are waiting for us.

Caleb wanted his mountain, even if there were giants on it. He trusted God to help him take it. We can do whatever God wants us to do. He will never ask us to do something we can't do with his help. Let's trust him to help us take our mountain and defeat our giants.

Word Search:
Bible Giants

Find and circle the following words taken from the facts and story about Bible giants. You can go down, across, and diagonally (but not backwards).

bed	foot	hand	six
Caleb	giants	iron	spies
Canaan	go (find 4 times)	Joshua	ten
cities	God	mountain	thirteen
David	grasshoppers	nine	toes
fingers	grow	Og (find 5 times)	two

```
O G C G O G M D A V I D T
G R A S S H O P P E R S H
I O N P O G U D O G C J I
A W A I R O N B E D I O R
N X A E X A T O E S T S T
T E N S H C A L E B I H E
S W S I X N I N E X E U E
F O O T F I N G E R S A N
```

13

A Perfect Little Lamb

Introduction

"The next day John saw Jesus coming toward him and said, 'Look! There is the Lamb of God who takes away the world's sin!'"

(John 1:29, TLB)

ONCE a little Chinese boy, Leland Wang, was very naughty. His mother got a stick in order to punish him, but Leland ran away. "Ha, ha, ha! You can't catch me!" he taunted her.

The mother knew he was too lively for her, so she stopped running and said, "I am ashamed that I have brought up a boy who isn't willing to be punished when he does wrong. I will have to punish myself." Then she beat her arm with the stick.

Leland ran to her, crying, "No, Mother, don't hurt yourself. Punish me." Do you suppose she punished him? No. By then there was no punishment for him because she had already taken it for him. She was his substitute. There is a substitute in today's Bible story—a little lamb.

The Facts, Please!

1. Sheep are mentioned in the Bible more than any other animal—about 750 times in all. They were an important part of the lives of people who lived in Bible times. Their wool was spun into cloth, and their meat was eaten. Sometimes sheepskins were worn for clothing. The horns were used as containers for carrying oil. A curved ram's horn, when cut off at the end, became a musical horn, which the Jews called a *shofar.*

2. Sheep are used in the Bible as object lessons to teach us about God and about ourselves. By nature, sheep often wander away from where they should be, unless they have someone to lead them in the right way. Because we are all sinners and have wandered away from God, we are like sheep that have gone astray.

3. God told the people of Old Testament times to offer an animal as a sacrifice when they sinned. A lamb was used most often. God said it had to be perfect, without any broken bones, spots, or other blemishes. Why? Because the lamb was a symbol for Jesus, who died in our place on the cross. He was perfect. He never sinned.

When a lamb was sacrificed, its blood was spilled. Without the shedding of blood, no sins were forgiven.

Bible Story: Blood on the Doorposts
(Exodus 11:1-10; 12:1-36)

One day Moses told Pharaoh, "The Lord God says, 'Let my people go to hold a feast to me in the wilderness.'"

The Israelites had been slaves in Egypt for 430 years. Pharaoh didn't want to lose all that free labor. "I don't know who the Lord is, and I won't let the people go," he snarled.

God sent nine terrible plagues to the Egyptians. Still, Pharaoh refused to let God's people leave.

Moses gave Pharaoh one last message: "One night soon, at midnight, God will come into Egypt, and all the firstborn of man and beast will die."

Moses told the Israelites, "Each family must take a male lamb of one year and pen it up. It must be perfect, without any blemishes. On the fourth day, kill your lamb and put its blood in a basin. Dip a bunch of hyssop in the blood and sprinkle it on the sides and top of your doorposts. When God comes into Egypt, your sons will not die."

On the fourth night, the Israelites waited inside their houses, with the blood on the doorposts. At midnight, not one of their firstborn children died. But in Egyptian homes there was a great wailing for the dead. Just imagine what it was like in Pharaoh's palace. He was awakened by screams. He grabbed a torch and ran toward his oldest son's room. On his way, he saw some of his guards lying dead on the floor. He entered his son's room and cried out, "He's dead! My son is dead!"

Pharaoh sent for Moses. "Please leave us—all of you," he demanded. That very night the Israelite slaves started on their long journey to the Promised Land. They were free!

This Is for You

We are like sheep that have gone astray. All of us are, for we have all sinned. God loves us very much, but he hates sin. He must punish the sinner, even though he doesn't want to do it. That's why he sent his Son to be our substitute.

Jesus, the perfect sinless Lamb, took our place when he suffered and died on the cross. He shed his blood to wash away our sins. Now he is alive, and he wants to come into our heart and forgive our sins. He will not force his way into our heart, though. He waits for us to ask him to save us.

If the Egyptians had put the blood on their doorposts, no one would have died. How can we escape God's judgment for our sins? By believing in Jesus as our Savior. His blood will wash away our sins. Have you done that? If not, will you do it now?

Our Substitute

Fill in the blanks in the sentences. Find those words in the puzzle and circle them. You can go horizontally, vertically, and diagonally.

J̲ __ __ __ __ came down from h̲ __ __ __ __ __ to

e̲ __ __ __ __ to be p̲ __ __ __ __ __ __ __ by dying on the

c̲ __ __ __ __ for o̲ __ __ s̲ __ __ __. He was laid in a

t̲ __ __ __. Because he is G̲ __ __, he a̲ __ __ __ __ from the

dead and went back u̲ __ to heaven and wore his

c̲ __ __ __ __ as King. What a S̲ __ v̲ __ __ __ Jesus is!

```
J  S  E  U  P  D  C  A
E  I  A  X  U  M  R  R
S  N  R  V  N  C  O  O
U  S  T  X  I  R  S  S
S  L  H  D  S  O  S  E
T  O  M  B  H  W  R  O
H  E  A  V  E  N  K  U
Z  J  G  O  D  T  Q  R
```

Supper's Ready!

Introduction

"For every time you eat this bread and drink this cup you are retelling the message of the Lord's death, that he has died for you. Do this until he comes again."

(1 Corinthians 11:26, TLB)

HERE is a description of an American holiday. What date is it? American flags are flying. There are parades with marching bands and servicemen in uniform. People are having picnics and listening to politicians' speeches. And at night, there are big fireworks displays. Did you guess the Fourth of July—the date when we celebrate our nation's birthday? It is called Independence Day because on that day in 1776 our forefathers signed the Declaration of Independence.

The Jewish people have a national birthday, too—a time

when they celebrate their independence and their beginning as the nation of Israel. God told them to celebrate it each year with a special supper, called Passover.

The Facts, Please!

1. The name *Passover* reminded the Israelites of the night in Egypt when the Lord "passed over" their houses because they had put blood on their doorposts. In their slavemasters' houses, where there was no blood, the oldest son died. That night Pharaoh let the Israelites leave Egypt. They were free!

2. After that, God told the Israelites to celebrate Passover once a year in the spring at the time of the full moon. At this special supper, certain things were eaten:
   - A roasted lamb—This was a year-old male that was perfect, without any defects. It was taken to the temple, where it was killed. Its fat was burned, and its blood was offered on the altar. Then it was taken home and roasted.
   - Unleavened bread—This was bread that had no leaven in it. It was eaten at Passover and for the next week. Leaven is like yeast, which causes bread to rise. Unleavened bread is thin and hard. When the Israelites escaped from Egypt, the women didn't have time to bake raised bread, so they ate this instead.
   - Bitter herbs—This was wild lettuce, or something similar. It reminded the Israelites of the bitterness of slavery.

- A sauce—This was called *charoseth*. It was a paste of dried dates, raisins, and vinegar, and was about the color of a brick.

     (Do you remember that the Jewish slaves in Egypt made bricks?)
- Red wine—A drink made from the juice of grapes.

Bible Story: A Special Supper
(Exodus 12:1-36)

(In the following story, the characters are fictional, but they celebrate Passover as it was done when Jesus was on earth.)

One spring day Jacob and Martha sat on the flat rooftop of their home in Jerusalem. "I hope Uncle Josiah and his family get here soon," said Martha. "I want to see Simon and Joanna."

"Me, too," replied Jacob. "The moon is full tomorrow night, and they will help us celebrate our special supper. Oh, look! I see Uncle Josiah now. They're here!"

That evening Father searched all through the house for leaven. "Not one tiny bit of it must be here," he said. "We will eat only unleavened bread for one week."

On Passover morning Father burned the leaven he had found. Then he and Uncle Josiah, with Simon and Jacob, took a lamb to the temple, where its blood was offered on the altar. When they returned home, the women and girls had a fire ready. The lamb was roasted on a spit of pomegranate wood.

In the evening everyone sat at the table for the Passover supper. Father asked a blessing. Then each person ate some unleavened bread, dipped in the charoseth. They ate a small amount of the bitter herbs and, last of all, the roasted lamb. During the meal, they took sips of wine. Sometimes they stopped for prayers of thanksgiving.

"Father, what is the meaning of this service?" asked Jacob when Father nodded to him. "How is this night different from all others?" Then Father took a long time telling the story about the night when God passed over the Israelites' houses, and they escaped from Egypt.

Martha gave a happy sigh and said, "I'm proud that I'm an Israelite and worship the only true God of heaven and earth!" And the rest of the family agreed.

This Is for You

The Passover celebrated the beginning of the Jewish nation. God knew that it looked forward to something even more wonderful—a time when Jesus would die on the cross for the sins of the world. The lamb who shed its blood is a picture of that.

We have a supper of celebration, too. It is the Lord's Supper (the Lord's Table and Communion are other names for this celebration). The bread is a picture of Jesus' body that was broken when the nails pierced it. The cup is a picture of his blood that he shed. When we take part in this special supper, we look back to Jesus' death on the cross for our sins.

If you're a Christian, do you take the Lord's Supper thoughtfully, thanking Jesus for dying for you? Do you praise him for your second birthday, when you were born again? Are you proud to be a child of the only true God of heaven and earth?

Scrambled Words:
An Invitation to the Passover Celebration

This is a letter Jacob might have written to his cousin, Simon, inviting him and his family to the Passover Feast. Some of the words are scrambled. Unscramble them to learn what Jacob's letter said.

Dear Simon,

It is a lovely GINPRS _____ day here in RELEMAJUS

_____. Soon there will be a LUFL OMON

_____ _____ and we will celebrate SOPAREVS

_____. Father has asked me to write and invite

you and your family to visit us during all the days of the

STEAF _____ of NUEEELAVND DRAEB

_____ _____. We have already picked out

a special MABL _____ to be CARIFDICES

_____ and STOARED _____ for our

PURSEP _____. We will have unleavened DRAEB

_____, bitter RHEBS _____, and charoseth ECAUS

_____. How happy it will make all of us if you can

come!

Your cousin,
Jacob

Two Huge Loaves of Bread

Introduction

"By him therefore let us offer the sacrifice of praise to God continually, that is, the fruit of our lips giving thanks to his name."

(Hebrews 13:15, KJV)

DON'T you just hate it? You do something special for someone, but that person doesn't even thank you. Although you didn't do it for thanks or praise, you would like to know that the person appreciated your thoughtfulness.

Many verses in the Bible tell us that God wants to be thanked and praised for his goodness to us. He commanded the Israelites to keep a special day of thanksgiving. It was the Feast of Harvest.

The Facts, Please!

1. The Feast of Harvest was held 50 days after Passover. Another name for it was the Feast of Pentecost. The Jews celebrated it at the end of the barley harvest, during the time they were harvesting their wheat.

2. Two huge loaves of bread were baked for the celebration of the Feast of Harvest in the temple at Jerusalem. First, wheat was reaped from a small field. It was hauled to the threshing floor in an ox cart. There the grain was spread out on the floor, and small oxen pulled a threshing board over it. Next the wheat was winnowed by tossing it into the air with a wooden fork and letting the wind blow away the chaff (light hulls). The remaining chaff was removed by shaking the grains through a big sieve.

3. The wheat was ground into flour between two round flat stones. God instructed that one-fifth of a bushel of fine flour was to be used for making each large loaf.

4. At a special ceremony in the temple, the priests "waved" the loaves. That is, they passed them before the altar as an offering to the Lord.

Bible Story: A Happy March to Jerusalem
(Exodus 23:14-19; Leviticus 23:15-21; Deuteronomy 16:9-12)

(In the following story, the characters are fictional,

but they show how real people celebrated the Feast of Harvest.)

"I can hardly believe it, Joanna," said Simon. "It has already been 50 days since we went to Jerusalem for Passover. Now we are going again, this time to celebrate the Feast of Harvest. I helped Father prepare our gift of grain to take."

"Oh, it will be such a happy time!" Joanna exclaimed.

That evening, many people from nearby villages walked to a larger town, where they camped outside its walls. Before sunrise, the watchman in a tower on the city wall cried out loudly, "Arise! Let us go up to Zion unto the Lord our God!"

Soon a happy crowd marched to the sound of trumpets and flutes. Simon and Joanna joined with the others as they sang songs of thanksgiving for the harvest. They climbed a hilltop, and there lay the city of Zion—Jerusalem. At its gates, the rulers welcomed them. "Enter in peace," they said.

Great crowds of people marched through the narrow streets and up to the temple. Mother and Joanna stayed in the Court of Women, while Father and Simon went into the Court of Israel. There the priests accepted all the gifts for the Lord. Simon watched as they took the huge loaves of bread and waved them before the altar and sacrificed lambs and goats. Together, all the men and boys thanked God for his goodness to them.

Later, at their feast, the people invited those who had no food to eat with them. And everyone sang together, "Blessed be the Lord God, the God of Israel, who only doeth good things."

This Is for You

What is the only thing we can give to God that he didn't first give to us? Our time? Our talents? Our money? Of course we will want to give him some of each of these, but when we do, we are giving back what he has already given us. There is one thing we can give him that comes from us alone. It is our praise—thanks to him for his goodness to us. And that should be the easiest thing of all to give!

When we feel upset or worried, let's start thinking about the good things God has given us. There are so many! Then let's thank him for them. We can thank him that he is going to answer our prayers and meet our needs in the way that is best for us. Praising the Lord drives the blues away and makes the Lord happy, too.

Praise the Lord

Look up the verses in Psalm 148 in your Bible and finish the words.

Who or what should praise the Lord? (Psalm 148)

Verse 2: A _ _ _ _ _

Verse 3: S _ _, M _ _ _, S _ _ _ _

Verse 4: H _ _ _ _ _ _ _ (S _ _ _ _ _—TLB)

Verse 9: M _ _ _ _ _ _ _ _ _, H _ _ _ _,

F _ _ _ _ T _ _ _ _, C _ _ _ _ _

Verse 11: K _ _ _ _ _

Verse 12: <u>Y</u> _ _ _ _   <u>M</u> _ _,   <u>M</u> _ _ _ _ _ _,

<u>O</u> _ _   <u>M</u> _ _,   <u>C</u> _ _ _ _ _ _ _

Are you named here? Do you remember to praise the
Lord? On the lines below, name some things the Lord has
given you that you can thank him for.

_____

_____

16

An Unusual Camping Shelter

Introduction

"I will remember the deeds of the Lord; yes, I will remember your miracles of long ago. I will meditate on all your works and consider all your mighty deeds."

(Psalm 77:11-12)

Do you like to look at pictures in family albums of your relatives who lived and died long before you were ever born? Ask your parents or grandparents to tell you some stories about these ancestors of yours, if they can.

God wanted the Jewish children to know about how he had taken care of their ancestors when they lived for 40 years in the desert. So he told the Israelites to have a camping holiday so they would tell their children stories about this time. This holiday was called the Feast of Tabernacles.

While they celebrated it, the people lived in unusual camping shelters.

The Facts, Please!

1. The Feast of Tabernacles was held in the fall, after the whole harvest had ended with the picking of the grapes. It was a time of thanksgiving for the harvest. It was also a time to remember the stories of how God took care of their ancestors in the desert for 40 years.

2. This feast lasted for a week. All who could traveled to Jerusalem for the celebration. Everyone lived in shelters, or booths, for seven days. This was to remind them that the Israelites lived in tents during their long stay in the desert.

3. The shelters were made by nailing a three-sided wooden framework to four poles, with the fourth side left open for a doorway. A top was added, also. Over the framework were laid branches and leaves of palm, cedar, willow, and olive trees. The rule was that there must be enough space between the leaves that the stars might be seen.

4. The shelters were built on the flat rooftops, in courtyards, or in gardens.

Bible Story: Let's Go Camping!
(Leviticus 23:33-44)

(In the following story, the characters are fictional,

but they show how real people celebrated the Feast of Tabernacles.)

"Welcome to Jerusalem, Simon and Joanna," said Jacob. "We are glad you can celebrate the Feast of Tabernacles with us."

"We could hardly wait for you to get here," added Martha. "Mother and I have been cooking good food. There are loaves of wheat bread, cakes of barley, and many sweet cakes. We roasted lambs and made butter and cheese, too."

Simon and Jacob helped their fathers build the camping shelters in the garden. For a shelter, they dug four holes in the ground and put poles in them. Jacob enjoyed helping nail the lattice framework to the poles. Simon liked to weave the tree boughs with their fragrant green leaves in the lattice.

The children especially enjoyed marching behind a priest each morning as he went to the Pool of Siloam with a golden pitcher. The priest dipped the pitcher into the pool and filled it with water to the brim. Then the whole procession marched back to the temple. The Levites blew three blasts on silver trumpets as they entered the temple gate. The priest went inside to the altar, where he poured out the water.

Each night Jacob said, "Father, tell us some more stories about why we celebrate the Feast of Tabernacles." Then his father would tell how God had taken care of the Israelites in the wilderness. For 40 years God had given them food and water, and the people's clothes and shoes did not wear out.

"Don't forget these stories," Father said. "When you have some special needs, remember that the same God who took care of your ancestors will provide for you, too."

Later, when four sleepy children lay in their shelters and looked up at the stars, they thanked God that he was their God and would always take care of them.

This Is for You

The Old Testament was not written just so we could know the history of Bible days. The stories about people who lived back then teach us that God is faithful and that we can count on him to do what he says. He took care of them, and he will take care of us. He hated their sin and punished them if they didn't turn from it. When they did turn from sin, he blessed them. He will do the same for us.

We can't remember something we never learned in the first place. That's why we should read and study the Bible. Then, when we are in a scary situation, we can remember how God cared for Daniel in the lions' den or helped someone else in danger. When we have a special need, we can remember how God provided food and water in the desert for the Israelites. The stories of Bible people can help us to trust God now, in our lifetime, for the same God that took care of them will help us, too.

Match-Up:
The Israelites' Special Camping Trip

Draw a line from the first part of each sentence to its correct ending.

1. Every year the Israelites had a special camping trip to celebrate the

   the harvest.

2. It was held in the

   tree limbs and leaves.

3. It was a time of thanksgiving for

   the Pool of Siloam.

4. Everyone lived in shelters (booths) for

   tents.

5. This reminded them that for 40 years the Israelites lived in the desert in

   food and water.

6. The shelters were made of four poles and a framework into which were woven

   fall.

7. In Jerusalem the priests led a procession to get water from

   clothes and shoes.

8. For 40 years in the desert God provided the hungry and thirsty people with

   seven days.

9. In all those years the people did not need new

   Feast of Tabernacles.

Money Bags with Holes

Introduction

"Seek ye first the kingdom of God, and his righteousness; and all these things shall be added unto you."

(Matthew 6:33, KJV)

A long time ago, when a nickel would buy a large candy bar, a little girl started out for Sunday school. "Here are two nickels," said her mother. "One is for your gift to God at church. With the other, you may buy a candy bar on the way home."

The little girl held the money in her hand as she skipped along to church. On the way, she dropped her two nickels. One rolled through a sewer grate and disappeared. "Uh-oh!" she exclaimed. "There goes God's nickel!"

Whom did the little girl put first—God or herself? The

Israelites in Haggai's day put themselves first. Because of this, they lost their money—not through a grate, but through a money bag with holes.

The Facts, Please!

1. In the earliest of Bible times, trade was done through barter (the exchange of one article for another without the use of money). If an article is exchanged for money, then you aren't bartering, but selling.

2. A medium of exchange became necessary when ancient people stopped being nomadic hunters and began to settle down in an agricultural system. Then they would trade something they owned for something they needed or wanted. For instance, King Solomon traded wheat and olive oil for the cypress trees he used in building the temple.

3. The use of money in exchange for items began when some authority decided that gold, silver, or other metals would stand for the value of goods. When metals were first used for exchange, they were just weighed quantities of metal. These could be in the shape of discs, bars, or rings.

4. The earliest known coin was used about 700 B.C. The earliest coins mentioned in the Bible are gold ones called *drams*.

5. The shaped metals or coins were often carried in money bags. A girdle (a waistband of leather) sometimes had a slit into which money or other valuables

were put. Other times a person carried a small bag for this purpose.

Bible Story: Where, Oh Where Has My Money Gone?
(Haggai 1:1-15; 2:15-19)

The beautiful temple that King Solomon had built in Jerusalem was in ruins, destroyed by the armies of King Nebuchadnezzar of Babylon. He also took the Israelites as captives to Babylon. Why? God allowed his people to be captured because they worshiped idols, not God.

After many years, King Cyrus let a few of the Israelites return to their land to rebuild the temple. They began the work, laying the foundation of the altar. Then they said, "It isn't the time to build the house of God." Instead, they built fine homes for themselves.

After 15 years, God sent the prophet Haggai to preach to them. He said, "God says, 'Is it time for you to live in your fine homes, when my temple lies in ruins? You'd better think about your ways. You plant many crops, but you harvest only a few. You have hardly enough clothes to wear and food to eat. You earn money, but it disappears as though you had put it into a bag with holes. When you bring home money, I blow it away. Why? Because my temple is in ruins, and you don't care.'"

"God is holding back the rain and keeping your crops from producing, he has sent rust and mildew and hail," Haggai went on. "If you want him to bless you, climb the mountains, bring the wood, and build God's house." Twenty-three days later, the people began to rebuild the temple. God didn't even wait for them to finish. He said, "From this day on, I will bless you." Soon the rains came, the crops grew, and they had plenty.

This Is for You

The Israelites put their own houses ahead of God's temple. They chose to place themselves first and God second. That's why he didn't bless them. Without his rain, their crops failed. They earned money, but it seemed to disappear, like putting money in a bag with holes. When they finally went to work and rebuilt the temple, God sent them blessings right away.

It is very easy for us to put other things ahead of God. Maybe we are doing that without realizing it. Decide what you would do in these situations:

1. On Wednesday night there is a basketball game you want to see at your school, but that's the night your youth group meets. 2. You want to go to a friend's house, but your parents want you to baby-sit for them so they can visit guests at your church. 3. You have saved $5.00 for tithe and $5.00 to buy something you want very much. The item turns out to cost $7.50. Would you take $2.50 of your tithe money to buy it?

What did you choose? Can you tell by your choices if God has first place in your life? If God is first in these and other choices that you face, he will bless you and give you lasting joy. If he isn't first, sooner or later you'll find yourself "putting your money into a bag with holes."

Coded Message:
Mending the Holey Bags

To find the answer to each question, fill in each blank with the letter that comes after the letter found below each line. A will follow Z.

Why did the Israelites' money seem to disappear as though it were in a bag with holes?

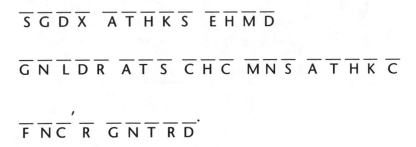

$\overline{}\ \overline{}\ \overline{}\ \overline{}$ $\overline{}\ \overline{}\ \overline{}\ \overline{}\ \overline{}$ $\overline{}\ \overline{}\ \overline{}\ \overline{}$
S G D X   A T H K S   E H M D

$\overline{}\ \overline{}\ \overline{}\ \overline{}\ \overline{}$ $\overline{}\ \overline{}\ \overline{}$ $\overline{}\ \overline{}\ \overline{}$ $\overline{}\ \overline{}\ \overline{}$ $\overline{}\ \overline{}\ \overline{}\ \overline{}$
G N L D R   A T S   C H C   M N S   A T H K C

$\overline{}\ \overline{}\ \overline{}$' $\overline{}$ $\overline{}\ \overline{}\ \overline{}\ \overline{}\ \overline{}$.
F N C   R   G N T R D

What did they do to cause God to "mend" their holey bags and begin to bless them?

$\overline{}\ \overline{}\ \overline{}\ \overline{}$ $\overline{}\ \overline{}\ \overline{}\ \overline{}\ \overline{}$ $\overline{}\ \overline{}$ $\overline{}\ \overline{}\ \overline{}\ \overline{}$
S G D X   A D F Z M   S N   A T H K C

$\overline{}\ \overline{}\ \overline{}$' $\overline{}$ $\overline{}\ \overline{}\ \overline{}\ \overline{}\ \overline{}$.
F N C   R   G N T R D

18

Sunk in a
Muddy Dungeon

Introduction

"Blessed are you when people insult you, persecute you
and falsely say all kinds of evil against you because of
me. Rejoice and be glad, because great is your reward in
heaven, for in the same way they persecuted the prophets who were before you."

(Matthew 5:11-12)

In an Indian village in Mexico, a Christian man named
Antonio was called before the village council. The chief sat
in the center of the room, surrounded by several men with
guns. "You must give up your new religion or leave this village," demanded the chief. "Choose one or the other, or my
men will shoot you."

"I can't give up Jesus, and I can't leave my village until I have told everyone else about him," replied Antonio.

Months passed. Antonio's life was full of persecution and danger. Still, he kept on witnessing. Today there is a little church in the village and a group of believers—all because one faithful Indian man loved Jesus more than his own life.

The prophet Jeremiah was faithful, too, even when he was put into a muddy dungeon.

THE FACTS, PLEASE!

1. The kind of dungeon in which Jeremiah was imprisoned was a cistern—a large hole dug for storing water.

2. Primitive people located their homes near water in rivers, ponds, or springs. Later, they learned to dig wells. Cisterns were built where there was no water source for the wells.

3. Cisterns were often needed in Palestine because there is very little rainfall there from May to September. In the rainy months, people stored up rainwater for dry months.

4. The first cisterns were dug out of soft limestone rock, which often broke open. About the time the Israelites conquered Canaan, a better cistern was developed by sealing the walls and bottom with waterproof plaster.

5. In the dry season, a cistern might be used as a prison when the water was all used up. Inside, the bottom was dark and damp and sometimes full of mud.

Bible Story: Up to His Armpits in Mud
(Jeremiah 37–38)

It was an awful time in the land of Judah. King Nebuchadnezzar had taken most of the people to live in Babylon. Now he had returned with his armies to capture the remaining Jews. Even then, they and their wicked king, Zedekiah, didn't turn to God. Jeremiah told them, "God is punishing you. He says you must surrender to Nebuchadnezzar."

"You're a traitor!" accused some of the young princes. They flogged Jeremiah and shoved him into a dungeon under a house. After a few days, King Zedekiah took him out and kept him in the palace prison.

Jeremiah didn't let persecution stop him. From prison, he sent out warnings: "Obey God. Don't fight Nebuchadnezzar!"

Again the princes seized Jeremiah. This time, they threw him in a cistern in the prison yard. He sunk into the gooey, slimy mud. Without food and water, he would die of starvation.

Ebed-Melech, an officer of the court, said to Zedekiah, "They have put Jeremiah in a cistern. He will die there."

"Take 30 men with you and get Jeremiah out," the king ordered.

Ebed-Melech dropped some old rags down to Jeremiah. "Put the rags under your armpits to protect them from the ropes," he said. "Tie the ropes under your arms, and we will pull you up." When he was ready, the men yanked hard on the ropes. Slowly, Jeremiah came up out of the cistern.

Jeremiah's words from God came true. King Nebuchadnez-zar captured Jerusalem and burned it, leaving nothing but a pile of blackened stones and ashes. He took Zedekiah hostage and killed his sons in front of him. Then he put out the king's eyes and took him and most of the people to Babylon.

This Is for You

For 40 years, Jeremiah faithfully gave God's messages to the Jews. Judah's leaders persecuted him again and again. He was beaten, threatened, and imprisoned. Still, he kept on doing what God wanted him to do. And he received rewards in heaven for his faithful service.

God wants all of his followers to be faithful, even to death. He expects us to keep on serving him, no matter what happens. He doesn't guarantee that we won't have troubles and persecution for being true to him. But he does promise to be with us all through our life and to give us strength to do what he wants. Best of all, he says that we will receive rewards in heaven. When we're there and can see Jesus, we'll say, "I wish I had done more for my wonderful Savior."

Jeremiah in the Dungeon

Fill in the missing letters in the words of the sentences. Then find and circle those words in the puzzle. You can go horizontally, vertically, or diagonally.

1. Nebuchadnezzar was the k _ _ _ of Babylon who fought against God's people, the J _ _ _ , and their king, Zedekiah.

2. Jeremiah was a p _ _ _ _ _ _ t who t _ l _ God's message to the Jews.

3. Jeremiah said, "G _ _ wants you to surrender to Nebuchadnezzar."

4. The Jews called him a t _ _ _ _ _ _ and put him in a c _ _ _ _ _ _ with deep m _ _ in the bottom.

5. Zedekiah let Ebed-Melech rescue Jeremiah. Ebed-Melech gave Jeremiah old r _ _ _ for under his a _ _ _ _ _ _ and pulled him up with r _ _ _ _ .

6. Nebuchadnezzar and his ar _ _ _ _ captured Jerusalem and burned it down. Zedekiah and most Jews were taken to Babylon.

7. God took care of Jeremiah, because he was tr _ _ and faithful to God.

```
A R M P I T S T O
R R T R A I T O R
M K O O T X Q L A
I I Z P G R M D G
E N X H E O U C S
S G J E W S D E Q
C I S T E R N X V
```

19

A Plumb Line and a Crooked Wall

Introduction

"All scripture is given by inspiration of God, and is profitable for doctrine, for reproof, for correction, for instruction in righteousness."

(2 Timothy 3:16, KJV)

Suppose you wanted to build a brick wall for an expensive house. You would choose bricks made from the finest clay. They would be held together with the best cement mortar. But if your wall is not absolutely in line, if it bulges out in any spot, the whole wall could collapse. Is there a simple way to check your work as you go along? Yes. There is a device called a plumb line.

Suppose you wanted to buy a beautiful old brick house. Because of its age, you would probably want to know if the walls were still straight and true. How could you find out? Again, you could use a simple plumb line.

The Facts, Please!

1. A plumb line is a cord with a lead weight, or plumb, on one end. It is used to determine vertical direction. Because of the earth's gravity, the plumb will hold the cord straight and perpendicular to the earth. The plumb, sometimes called the plumb bob, is egg- or pear-shaped and comes to a point. When held alongside a brick wall, a plumb line will show whether the wall is crooked or straight.

2. Plumb lines have been in use at least as far back as the early work of masons in Egypt. King Menes of Egypt is known to have used them in about 2900 B.C. They are mentioned in the Bible in several Old Testament Scriptures.

3. Even today, masons constantly use a plumb line to determine if they are building a wall straight and true. This device is also used to determine if an old wall is still straight.

4. When King Solomon died, the nation of Israel was divided into two parts—the northern kingdom (Israel) and the southern kingdom (Judah). Our last story told how Judah was captured by the Babylonians because of idol worship. But even before that, the northern kingdom of Israel had turned from God to idols. So God sent a preacher to tell them that he was measuring

them with a plumb line. Why did he say that? They were not a brick wall. God meant that he was checking them out to see if they were staying true to him.

Bible Story: Straighten Up, Crooked Israel!
(Amos 7:7-17)

In the farmlands of Judah, six miles south of Bethlehem, lived a poor man named Amos. He herded sheep and gathered figs from wild sycamore trees. Through the long, quiet days of looking after the sheep, Amos probably thought about God and his commandment "You shall have no other gods before me." He was sad because many Israelites were worshiping idols. They were breaking the very first of God's Ten Commandments.

One day God spoke to Amos: "Go and prophesy to my people Israel." Amos loved God. He didn't ask why he chose him, a poor herdsman, to preach. He left his sheep and went to Israel. "God gave me a vision that he wants me to tell you about," Amos told the Israelites. "I saw the Lord standing beside a wall with a plumb line in his hand. He said, 'Amos, what do you see?' I answered, 'I see a plumb line.'

"And the Lord said, 'I will test my people with a plumb line. I will no longer hold off their punishment. The idol altars and temples of Israel will be destroyed, and with my sword I will go against the house of King Jeroboam.'"

Amaziah, the priest of the golden calves, said to Amos, "Get out of here, you prophet! Go back to Judah where you came from! Prophesy there and don't bother us!"

111

"I was not a prophet, and I didn't go to the school of the prophets," Amos replied. "I herded sheep and picked wild figs. The Lord sent me here to prophesy. He has told me that you will have much trouble in your family, and Israel will be carried away captive to another land because of all the sin."

Amos's prophesies came true about 30 or 40 years later. The armies of Assyria swarmed over Israel's land, destroyed the capital city, and took the people captive.

This Is For You

A crooked wall will collapse sooner or later. Our life will, too, without a plumb line—something to tell us what is right and wrong. God's plumb line for our life is the Bible.

How can we use the Bible to measure our life? First of all, we must believe that God's Word is all true. In 2 Timothy 3:16, God says that all Scripture is inspired, which means "God-breathed," so we know it's true. We have many proofs that God wrote every word of the Bible.

God's Word is useful for doctrine (the truth about what is right), for reproof (showing us where we are out of line with what's right, just as a plumb line shows when a wall is out of line), for correction (showing us how to get back in line with what's right), and for instruction in righteousness (telling us how to stay in line with what's right).

Do we read and study the Bible? Do we use it as a plumb line to check our thoughts, our words, and our actions? When we do, God will show us when we are wrong and help us get in line with what's right and stay there. Let's always read our Bibles!

Staying in Line with the Bible

We have many Scriptures that apply to our life today. Under the crooked wall are listed some mistakes a young person might make. Look up the Bible verses listed under the straight wall and draw a line from each one to the mistake it is warning us about.

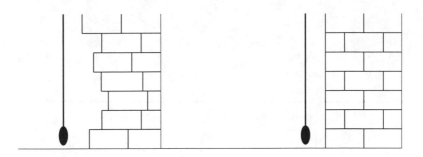

Talking back to parents

Stealing or cheating

Complaining about going to church

Not praying when tempted to sin

Disobeying parents

Cursing

Not reading and studying the Bible

Loving to do worldly things

Lying

Psalm 122:1

2 Timothy 2:15

Ephesians 6:1

Exodus 20:15

1 John 2:15

Ephesians 6:2

Ephesians 4:25

Exodus 20:7

Matthew 26:41

113

Sound the Alarm!

Introduction

"Remember this: Whoever turns a sinner from the error of his way will save him from death and cover over a multitude of sins."

(James 5:20)

WHEEEET! goes the shrill sound of the lifeguard's whistle at the beach. Then the guard lifts his megaphone to his lips and calls out, "Sharks! Sharks!" If you were swimming at that beach, would you swim for shore as fast as possible? You bet!

A lifeguard sits in a tower that is high enough for him to see swimmers and any dangers that lurk in the waters. When he sees the menacing fins of sharks nearby, a good lifeguard will warn the swimmers of the danger. Suppose he sees the danger, fails to give a warning, and a swimmer is bitten—or maybe even killed. Whose fault is it? If he gives a warning and that swimmer pays no attention, whose fault is it then?

The Facts, Please!

1. A lifeguard at the ocean has three things that help him see danger and give a warning: a high tower, a warning whistle, and his own alertness.

2. In Bible times, every Palestinian city or village had a watchman to warn of dangers that might be approaching, especially at night. Many watchmen were located in high towers, and they blew an alarm with a trumpet. Of course, like lifeguards today, they had to be alert and watchful.

3. Watchtowers in Bible times were high, fortified structures that enabled a watchman to see in every direction. Some were located at intervals on a city wall; others were on hilltops or other high places. Some watchtowers were equipped with military machines for throwing arrows and stones.

4. The Jews used a silver trumpet for sounding an alarm. The trumpets sounded different signals, depending on the situation.

5. The citizens of a city or village slept peacefully at night, for they depended on the watchman to warn them of danger. It was absolutely essential that the watchman stay alert, watching in all directions for

any sign of trouble. If he failed to do so, he could pay for it with his life.

Bible Story: Who Goes There?
(Ezekiel 3:16-21; 33:1-9)

(The first part of this Bible story is imaginary, but based on facts. The second part is true, as told in the Bible.)

As the sun set behind the Judean hills, Nemuel and Dorcas ate their evening meal with their children. "Prophet Jeremiah says the Babylonians are coming back to capture or kill those of us who are still here," said Nemuel. "But we will go to sleep tonight as usual. I think we're safe enough."

Eliab climbed up in his tower on the north side of the wall and scanned the horizon. All was quiet. He didn't see the Babylonian troops who were quietly surrounding the city. As darkness came on, they came closer. Suddenly, Eliab saw them. He put the trumpet to his lips and blew three long, loud blasts. The alarm awakened Dorcas and Nemuel. "Go back to sleep," Nemuel said. "Eliab probably saw some donkeys grazing." Soon the Babylonians entered their home and captured the whole family. On the south side of the city, another watchman saw some shadowy figures. He said to himself, "I'll wait to be sure it's the enemy." He dozed as the armies came into the city and killed or captured everyone. There had been no alarm.

In Babylon there lived a young prophet named Ezekiel, who had been captured in the Babylonians' second raid on the land of Judah. God told him, "You are to be a watchman to the house of Israel. When I give you a warning for my

117

people, you must pass my words on to them. If I say a wicked man will die because of his sins, and you don't warn him and give him a chance to repent, he will die in his sins. It will be your fault if he does. If you do warn him to repent and he doesn't, he will die in his sins, but it will be his fault—not yours."

Ezekiel was a good watchman for the Lord. He warned the people that God would punish them for their sins. Some repented of sins, and some didn't. But Ezekiel was not responsible when God punished them. He had sounded God's alarm loud and clear.

This Is for You

God told another prophet, Hosea, "Put a trumpet to your lips." He wanted Hosea to give a warning to the Jews that God's judgment was coming because of their sins. If we are Christians, God expects us to sound an alarm, too, warning sinners about Judgment Day. If Jesus comes or they die before they have trusted him as Savior, they will stand before him at the Great White Throne Judgment and will spend eternity in hell. It's not easy to be God's watchman and warn sinners to repent of sins and believe in Jesus as Savior. Some may laugh at us; others may avoid us and choose other friends. But if we fail to tell them about Jesus, they won't be able to live with him in heaven.

Not all people we witness to will be saved. But if we have tried to win them and they have refused Jesus, it's not our fault—it's their own. We can't give up our witnessing. Let's keep on sounding the alarm!

A Watchman and His Warning

From the list of words below, find the correct one to fill each blank. One word is used twice.

In Bible days, there were no _____ in the sky

to spy out enemy troop movements. There were no warn-

ing systems, using _____ or telephones to

alert the public of danger. But they did have a way to

warn people when danger approached. They had

_____ who stayed in _____ as

lookouts. If an enemy or any other kind of trouble

approached, they would blow an _____ with a

_____.

If a watchman sounded an alarm and the people did not

seek safety and then _____, it was their own

_____. If a watchman saw danger and didn't sound

an alarm, he was held _____ if people

died.

All Christians are to be God's _____, warning

sinners that they will stand before God on _____

_____ and spend eternity in _____ if they don't repent

119

and believe in _____ as _____. What kind of
watchman are _____?

alarm	Judgment Day	trumpet
died	responsible	watchmen
fault	satellites	watchtowers
hell	Savior	you
Jesus	televisions	

The Frightened Witch

Introduction

"God is our refuge and strength, an ever-present help in trouble. Therefore we will not fear, though the earth give way and the mountains fall into the heart of the sea."

(Psalm 46:1)

WHEN you grow up, what will you be? Will you get married? Will you have children? How many? Will your life be long or short? What is going to happen to you tomorrow? Are there certain things you should or should not do today?

All of us are curious about our future. We wonder what plans we should make for today or for later. Especially when we are afraid that something awful is going to happen, we wish we could know the future. Where do you turn for answers—a horoscope, a Ouija board, or a medium? Many

121

people do. King Saul used a witch (or medium) when he was in trouble.

The Facts, Please!

1. When witches are mentioned, some people think of black cats, broomsticks, and pointed hats. Others think of people who cast magic spells. Today, those who practice demonology and satanic worship call some of their leaders witches. In the Bible, if the term *witches* is used, it refers to sorcerers or mediums.

2. Mediums are people who claim they can tell the future by communicating with the spirits of dead people. The Bible gives us no indication that we can talk with people who have died. Those who claim they do this are either fooling people by some kind of tricks, or they are performing acts under the power of demons.

3. God told the Israelites to have nothing to do with fortune-tellers, black magic, witches, wizards, or sorcerers. In Exodus 22:18, God ordered witches (sorcerers) to be put to death.

4. King Saul obeyed that command at one time and tried to ban all the sorcerers from the land of Israel. Somehow, he missed at least one. Then there came a time when he wanted to talk with a sorcerer. Evidently, although he had obeyed God's command to ban witches, he still believed in witchcraft in his heart.

Bible Story: The Old Man Scares the Witch
(1 Samuel 28:3-25)

King Saul was in trouble. The armies of the Philistines were coming for another war against him. Saul rallied his forces together and set up camp. But when he saw the vast army of the Philistines, he was terrified. He prayed, "Lord, what shall I do?" But Saul received no answer because he had disobeyed God in the past. Saul would have gone to the prophet Samuel for help, but Samuel had recently died.

Saul didn't know where to turn. Finally, he said to his aides, "Find me a medium. I will go and inquire of her."

The aides told him there was a medium at Endor. Saul took off his royal robes, dressed in ordinary clothes, and went to the medium's house with two of his men. "There is a dead man I must talk to," he told the woman. "Please bring up his spirit."

"Saul has banned all mediums from the land," said the woman. "Why have you set a trap for me to be killed?" Saul promised that she would not be punished, so the medium asked, "Whom do you want to see?" Saul asked for Samuel.

Suddenly the woman screamed because she saw Samuel. "Why have you tried to fool me?" she asked the king. "You are King Saul!"

"Don't be frightened," said Saul. "I won't hurt you. What do you see?" The medium told him that she saw an old man, wrapped in a robe. Saul knew it was Samuel, and he bowed low.

"Why have you disturbed me, Saul?" Samuel asked.

"I am in great trouble," said Saul. "The Philistines are fighting against me, and God won't tell me what to do."

"Why do you bother asking God?" asked Samuel. "You turned away from him and made him your enemy. Now he will let the Philistines win the battle. Your kingdom will be given to David, and tomorrow you and your sons will be here with me."

Everything happened just as Samuel had said. The next day the Israelites were defeated, and Saul and his sons died. Soon after, David was made king of Israel.

This Is for You

Was the medium able to bring up Samuel's spirit by either her own or Satan's power? No. When she saw the old man, she screamed in fright. She hadn't really expected to see a spirit! God allowed Samuel to speak to Saul. This doesn't mean that God approves of using mediums—he still condemns them. But he allowed this to happen to let Saul know he was being punished for his sins.

Have you ever looked up your horoscope, just to see what it says about the day ahead? Have you played with a friend's Ouija board, thinking it was innocent fun? Perhaps you have attended an occult meeting out of curiosity. The devil is behind all these activities. Doing any of them can get you into serious trouble.

If you need special help, you can pray to God for help. He has all power and knows everything. He will guide you in the right paths. Why fool around with Satan?

Samuel Talks to Saul

Complete the acrostic by filling the blanks in these sentences from the story about Saul.

Saul <u>A</u> __ <u>K</u> __ __ God for help, but got no answer.

He <u>I</u> __ <u>Q</u> __ <u>I</u> __ __ __ of a medium, asking her

to <u>B</u> __ __ <u>N</u> __ up Samuel from the dead.

<u>G</u> __ __ brought up Samuel's spirit.

Seeing the <u>S</u> __ __ <u>R</u> __ __, the medium

screamed. Saul <u>A</u> __ <u>K</u> __ __ Samuel for help.

<u>S</u> __ __ <u>U</u> __ __ said that the

<u>I</u> <u>S</u> __ __ __ <u>L</u> __ __ __ __ would be defeated, and

Saul and his sons would die, and it was so!

22

God's Scales Weigh a King

Introduction

"Thou art weighed in the balances, and art found wanting. . . . For all have sinned, and come short of the glory of God."

(Daniel 5:27; Romans 3:23, KJV)

ONCE a very fat lady stepped on a scale to weigh herself. This scale showed a person's weight and also gave out a little card with a saying on it. The lady put in a coin, and out came a card with the words, "One at a time, please!"

Until you are fully grown, you may like to see your weight increasing. After a while, though, you begin to worry that you will get fat. A king had a different problem. He was too "skinny" when weighed on God's balance scales.

The Facts, Please!

1. A scale is a device for determining the weight of any substance. All types of weighing scales are based on the principle of balance.

2. The balance scale probably originated in ancient Egypt about five thousand years before Christ. The very first balance scales may have suspended a beam of wood by hanging it from a cord. Later, the cross-beam was supported in the middle by a vertical bar. Two pans of equal weight were hung on either end of the crossbeam.

3. A known weight was placed in one pan, and the object to be weighed was put in the other. By adding or subtracting known weights until both sides were balanced, the weight of the object could be learned. If a balance scale crossbeam tilts down on the side of the known weight, the object being weighed is too light. If it tilts the other way, the object is too heavy.

4. Balance scales are mentioned in several places in the Bible, going back to Job's and Moses' times. They are still in use today, with very little change.

Bible Story: The "Skinny" King
(Daniel 5)

One night King Belshazzar held a great banquet in his palace in Babylon for a thousand of his officers. After eating, they drank wine until they were very drunk. "I want to drink from the gold and silver cups that were brought here long ago from the temple in Jerusalem," Belshazzar said.

Soon the king, his wives, and the officers were drinking wine from the sacred cups that had once been used in the worship of the true God. Even worse, they raised the cups in the air and praised their false gods of gold, silver, iron, and wood.

Suddenly they saw the fingers of a man's hand writing on the plaster of the wall. The bright light of a nearby lampstand showed up the words very clearly. The king turned pale with fright, and his knees knocked together.

"Call for my astrologers and magicians!" Belshazzar ordered. "Whoever can read the writing and tell its meaning will be made third ruler in the kingdom, and I will give him a purple robe and a gold chain." When the magicians and astrologers couldn't tell what the writing meant, the king was even more terrified.

The queen mother rushed into the banquet hall. "There is a man in the kingdom who has the spirit and wisdom of the holy gods within him," she said. "Your father, King Nebuchadnezzar, made him chief of the wise men. His name is Daniel. He will tell you what the writing means."

When Daniel arrived, he said, "Your Majesty, the most high God gave King Nebuchadnezzar a kingdom and glory and honor. After a while, because he became very proud, God brought him down so low that he wandered in the fields and ate grass like an animal. When at last he knew that the most high God ruled in heaven, he was brought back to be king again. You knew all this, O king, yet you have not honored the true God.

"His fingers wrote the words on the wall, and he has told

me their meaning. This is it: *Mene*—the days of your kingdom are numbered and finished. *Tekel*—you are weighed in the balance and found wanting. *Peres*—your kingdom is divided and given to the Medes and Persians."

That very night, while the banquet was going on, Median soldiers slipped inside the walls of Babylon. Quietly, they surrounded the king's palace. Then they burst into the banquet hall, killed Belshazzar, and took over his kingdom. Their leader, Darius, became the new ruler of Babylon.

This Is for You

Belshazzar may have had a very fat body. When he was weighed on God's scales, though, he was "skinny." Because of his many sins, he did not measure up to what God expected him to be. He had heard about the true God, but he did not honor him.

How much do we weigh on God's scales? Nothing at all if we haven't become Christians. All people have sinned, and all of us come short of God's glory. That is, we don't measure up to God's glorious and perfect standard. Who does measure up? Only the Lord Jesus Christ. He never sinned.

God loves us and wants us to live with him in heaven. So he sent his Son to die on the cross in our place so we wouldn't have to suffer for our sins. If we will believe in him, his blood will wash away all our sin. Then, in God's sight, we will measure up—just as though we have never sinned at all. Are you too "skinny" on God's balance scales? If so, trust Jesus as your Savior today!

Coded Message:
Why was King Belshazzar "Skinny"?

To read the message about Belshazzar, write the letters under each number on the line where the number appears. Keep the letters in order and then separate them into words.

1 B	3 H	2 H	4 H	4 E	3 E	1 E	4 P	3 D	4 R
1 L	4 A	3 R	4 I	2 E	4 S	3 A	4 E	1 S	3 N
4 D	3 K	1 H	4 F	3 F	2 D	4 A	1 A	3 R	2 I
4 L	1 Z	3 O	4 S	2 D	1 Z	3 M	4 E	3 C	4 M
2 N	3 U	3 P	1 A	4 A	3 S	2 O	1 R	4 N	3 O
4 M	1 K	3 U	4 A	2 T	3 T	1 N	4 D	3 O	2 H
4 E	3 F	1 E	1 W	2 O	3 G	4 G	3 O	2 N	4 O
3 D	2 O	1 A	3 S	3 T	2 R	4 D	1 B	3 E	2 G
3 M	1 O	4 S	3 P	2 O	3 L	2 D	1 U	1 T	1 G
1 O	1 D	3 E							

1 _____

_____

2 _____

_____

3 _____

_____

4 _____

_____

Poisonous Gourds
for Supper

Introduction

"But the Holy Spirit tells us clearly that in the last times
some in the church will turn away from Christ and
become eager followers of teachers with devil-inspired
ideas."

(1 Timothy 4:1, TLB)

ONE time a father poured a liquid into a soft-drink bottle,
intending to use it for his work. One day he forgot to put it
away and left it on his garage floor. His little girl, thinking it
was a cola, took a drink and became violently ill. That harm-
less-looking liquid was poisonous! The girl was rushed to
the hospital and almost died before an antidote for the
poison could take effect.

In Bible times, people probably didn't know about antidotes, but one was needed when the prophet Elisha and his students ate poisonous wild gourds.

The Facts, Please!

1. Gourds grow on trailing or climbing vines and are closely related to squashes and pumpkins. They bear fruit of various colors and shapes. Some gourd vines are very fast-growing and may reach a height of 10 to 12 feet. Many types of wild gourds grew in the lands around the Mediterranean Sea in Bible times. Some could be eaten, and some were poisonous.

2. Poison is a substance that can cause sickness or death when it is eaten, drunk, or absorbed into the body. There are many kinds of poisonous plants. Fortunately, some of the most dangerous ones look, smell, or taste awful. Others may look very much like some edible food. (Poisonous mushrooms look much like mushrooms that are good food. A person who doesn't know the bad ones from the good ones should never pick and eat wild mushrooms.)

3. An antidote is a substance that can be taken to counteract the harmful effects of poison. It must be administered quickly after the poison has entered the body.

Bible Story: Death in the Pot
(2 Kings 4:38-41)

One day Elisha stood before his class of young

Bible students. It was almost suppertime, so he said to his servant, "Get out the big pot and make some stew."

There was a famine in the land, and food was hard to find. One of the young students went out to the fields to look for some vegetables to put in the stew. Seeing a wild vine, he picked some of its gourds and returned with a fold of his cloak filled with them. "Do you know what these are?" he asked the others. No one knew, but he shredded them up into the stew anyway.

"Supper's ready," called out the servant after a while. The men sat down, and each one had a big helping of stew.

After a few bites of food, the men cried out, "O man of God, there's death in the pot!" The stew must have tasted bitter. After they tasted it they knew that the gourds were poisonous and that they could all die!

"Quick! Bring me some flour," Elisha said. He threw the flour into the pot. "Serve this to the men," he told his servant. "It's all right now." The men ate the stew, and it did them no harm at all.

Was Elisha's flour an antidote for the poison? Not normally. He threw it in as an act of faith in God, trusting him to work a miracle and make the stew safe to eat. And he did! God used the flour to make the stew edible.

This Is for You

To be poisoned in our body is very bad, but there is something worse—to be poisoned in our mind. The devil wants to have us under his control. To do this, he tries to control our thinking. He wants us to believe that the Bible is out-of-date and that we must decide for ourself what we want to do with our life and how we want to act.

Satan has many helpers who teach his lies. Of course, these are not Christians, although some may claim to be. They may be teachers, government leaders, schoolmates, family members, or even pastors of churches. Whoever they are, if they teach anything that goes against what God's Word says, they are feeding us poison for our mind. It could ruin our life, both now and for eternity.

The Bible is like the flour that Elisha put in the pot of stew. It is God's antidote that he will use to help us recognize poisonous teachings when we hear them. If we read and study the Bible and believe it with all our heart, God will show us what is right and what is wrong. We can trust the teachings of those who are God's children and who believe the Bible.

The devil is working hard to poison the minds of young people these days. Don't let him poison yours!

False Teachings vs. God's Word

There are some dangerous false teachings these days that may be in your schoolbooks and classrooms. Some of these teachings are listed below. Draw a line from each one to the true statement from God's Word that matches it. Look up each verse as you do so.

False Teachings

The Truth from God's Word

Man is a Supreme Being; put faith and trust in man.

There is a devil (Satan). (1 Peter 5:8)

Man is an animal, having only a soul and body.

God is the Supreme Being; believe in him. (Isaiah 45:21-22)

There is no life after death.

All people have sinned. (Romans 3:23)

The earth and people came into being by evolution.

There is life after death. (1 Corinthians 15:52)

There is no such thing as sin.

God created the heavens and the earth. (Genesis 1:1)

There is no devil.

God made man in his image— body, soul, and spirit. (Genesis 1:27; 1 Thessalonians 5:23)

The Camel and the Eye of a Needle

Introduction

"Children, how hard it is for them that trust in riches to enter into the kingdom of God!"

(Mark 10:24, KJV)

ONCE a group of tourists in Egypt prepared for a trip to see the pyramids. All of them mounted their camels easily—all except a lady who weighed 350 pounds. Her camel knelt down for her to get on him. When she was settled, he got up part way, but her weight was too much for him. He collapsed down on his stomach, his feet spread out in all directions, and he let out a great big *oof!*

Over and over the poor camel tried to get up. Tired of waiting, the others in the tour went on to the pyramids. After a while, they saw the camel coming with the large lady on board. He was weaving from side to side, but he made it all the way to his destination. A most remarkable and useful animal indeed is the camel—the "ship of the desert."

The Facts, Please!

1. The Arabian camel, who lives in the vast deserts of Asia and North Africa, is a big animal. Except for the elephant, he is the largest animal trained and used by man in travel and work. He usually stands six feet tall at the shoulders, with his hump rising one foot above his back.

2. The camel's hump, which is his pantry, is made up of flesh and fat, weighing about 80 pounds. The fat is absorbed into his system when he is far out in the desert and cannot find any food. Water is stored in his stomach and released as needed. He has a tough, horny mouth that enables him to eat thorns from desert plants. His powerful teeth grind these up, and his stomach has the ability to digest them.

3. The camel has a thick padding on his knees, so he can kneel for people to mount him or load him with goods. His broad, two-toed foot, which is wide and well-padded, can walk across the hot desert sands easily. He can close his nostrils in a sandstorm to keep sand from getting into his nose. He also has a double row of bushy eyelashes that prevent sand from getting in his eyes in a sandstorm. With his keen sense of smell, he can locate water from far away in the desert.

4. In this Bible story Jesus talks about a camel and a needle's eye. The Bible mentions sewing as far back as Adam and Eve, who sewed fig leaves for a covering. Samples of needles found in archaeological digs have been made of iron, bone, or bronze and are similar to those of today.

Bible Story: A Poor Rich Man
(Mark 10:17-27)

One day a young man ran to Jesus and knelt down before him. "Good teacher," he said, "what must I do to have eternal life?"

"Why do you call me good?" asked Jesus. "There is no one who is perfectly good except God. You know the commandments: Don't kill, don't commit adultery, don't steal, don't lie, don't cheat, and honor your father and mother."

"Teacher, I have kept all these since I was a boy," boasted the young man.

Jesus, looking at the young man, loved him greatly. "There is just one more thing for you to do," he said. "Go and sell all your possessions and give to the poor, and you shall have treasure in heaven. Then take up your cross and come, follow me." Hearing this, the young man sadly bowed his head and walked away, for he was very rich.

Jesus watched him leave. "Children," he said to his disciples, "how hard it is for people who have riches to enter the kingdom of God!" The disciples were amazed. How could such a thing be? They thought that when a person had riches, it showed that he was especially blessed by God.

Jesus said again, "How hard it is for those who trust in

riches to enter the kingdom of God! It is easier for a camel to go through a needle's eye than for a rich man to be saved."

"Then who can be saved?" asked the disciples.

"With men it is impossible, but not with God," answered Jesus. "With God all things are possible."

This Is for You

The rich young man called Jesus good. That was the truth, but Jesus wanted him to understand that he is God, for only God is good. The man thought he must do something to become God's child. But he didn't know that good deeds won't save anybody. He said he had kept the commandments, but he failed to keep the first one: "Worship no other god before me." Money was the idol that he loved and trusted more than he did God.

Can a huge camel go through the eye of a sewing needle? Of course not! Neither can anyone be saved who trusts in riches or anything else instead of believing in Jesus for salvation.

Have you asked Jesus to save you? If not, why not? Are you afraid your friends will laugh at you? Do you think that being a Christian will keep you from having a good time? Are you trusting that you are good enough for heaven, just the way you are?

No matter what keeps you from Jesus, that is your idol. It is as if you are riding on that big old camel that can't get through the needle's eye. Get down and trust Jesus. He can do anything, and he will save you and make you his child right now.

Missing Letters:
How to Have Eternal Life

Write the missing letter from each set of letters from the alphabet on its line to find the word that finishes the sentence.

Sentence 1:

PQSTUV ____

HJKLMN ____

ABDEFG ____

CDEFGI ____

DFGHIJ ____

OPQRTU ____

The rich young ruler hoped to have eternal life by trusting in his _____.

Sentence 2:

FGHIKL ____

ABCDFG ____

RTUVWX ____

TVWXYZ ____

NOPQRT ____

The only way to have eternal life is by trusting in _____.

25

The Crushed Worm

Introduction

"Come, let's talk this over! says the Lord; no matter how
deep the stain of your sins, I can take it out and make
you as clean as freshly fallen snow. Even if you are
stained as red as crimson, I can make you white as wool!"

(Isaiah 1:18, TLB)

MANY years ago, a little girl named Mary wore her favorite
skirt to school one day. Mary had a bottle of permanent red
ink on top of her desk for filling her fountain pen.
(Ballpoint pens had not yet been invented.) As she
unscrewed the cap of the ink bottle, she dropped the bottle
in her lap. Very quickly, a huge red stain spread across the
front of her skirt. At home, her mother washed and scrub-

bed the stain, but it wouldn't come out. Mary never wore her pretty skirt again.

The Bible says our sins are like a crimson red stain that we can't remove. Who can? Before answering, let's think about a tiny worm.

The Facts, Please!

1. For many thousands of years man has improved the looks of fabrics, paper, leather, and other materials by coloring them with dyes. At first, there were only natural dyes, made from plants and animals. Later, man learned to make dyes from minerals of the earth. Today most dyes are man-made.

2. In Bible times dyes were made by preparing a solution of water, potash, and lime. After two days the colored pigments were added. The dyeing was done in stone basins or in earthenware pots. After that, the colored yarn or skin was rinsed in clear water and hung up to dry.

3. In Bible times there was a worm called the tola. It was a small grub the size of a pea. It got its nourishment by piercing plants like the oak. Swarms of these little worms were beaten off the plants and caught in a container. Then they were crushed. Their blood produced a brilliant crimson dye. It took the bodies of 70,000 worms to make one pound of the dye.

4. The dye from the tola worm was so difficult to make that crimson-colored clothes were too expensive for

anyone to buy, except those who were rich, great, or noble.

Bible Story: "I Am a Worm!"
(Psalm 22:6; Matthew 27:33-50)

One long-ago day on a hill called Golgotha there stood a wooden cross. A man was nailed to that cross, and over his head was a sign that read This Is Jesus, the King of the Jews. What? A king was being crucified? Yes, and he was not only the King of the Jews. He was the King of Glory— God.

What awful thing had this King done that he should die such a horrible death? Nothing. Nothing at all! He was perfect. He had never sinned. He was dying for the sins of the whole world. He was taking the punishment that everyone deserved.

Crucifixion was such a painful, shameful death that the Romans only hung slaves and criminals on crosses. Jesus' hands and feet were nailed to the cross. As he hung there, the soldiers and some of the Jews mocked him and laughed at him. He was hated and despised, as though he were the wickedest of men.

How did Jesus feel? God caused David to write the answer in Psalm 22:6: "I am a worm, and no man: a reproach of men, and despised of the people" (KJV). Jesus felt like the lowliest of creatures—a worm. The word he used for worm was *tola*—the tiny grub that was crushed to death so its blood could make the crimson dye. The King of Glory—the Lord of lords—felt like a worm! He could stoop no lower than that to save us.

After six long hours of agony, Jesus died. But, because he

is God, he rose again. Now the one who was made to feel like a worm reigns as King of kings and Lord of lords in heaven, and we will see him on his throne someday, if we're his children.

This Is for You

The Bible says our sins are red like crimson. We are stained with sin and cannot remove the stains, no matter what we do. Jesus was despised like a lowly worm. The tola was crushed to death to provide crimson robes. Jesus died so that our sins, as red as crimson, could be washed away, and we could be made whiter than snow or the whitest wool.

With his blood, Jesus paid the price to give us a white robe of salvation. Now he offers it to us free of charge. Are you dressed in your robe? Do you love him enough to ask him to come into your heart and forgive your sins?

Crossword Puzzle:
The Tola Worm and the King of Glory

What do the tola worm and the King of Glory, Jesus, have in common? To find out, fill in the blanks as you solve the crossword puzzle.

There is a w_____ called the t_____ that is c_____
         (1 down)   (4 across)   (6 down)
so that its b_____ can be made into a c_____
         (5 across)   (6 across)
d_____. Psalm 22:6 says that Jesus felt like a worm, not a
  (7 across)

148

m_____, when he d_____ for our s_____. He was
(8 down)   (13 across)   (14 across)
mocked and l_____ at, even though he is the King of
(2 across)
G_____. The tola worm gave its blood to provide crimson
(3 down)
robes. Jesus died to give us r_____ of s_____
(9 down)   (10 across)
that are as white as s_____. Isn't his l_____ wonderful?
(12 down)   (11 down)

A Sleepy General, a Bottle of Milk, and a Tent Peg

Introduction

"Whatsoever thy hand findeth to do, do it with thy might. . . . For it is God which worketh in you both to will and to do of his good pleasure."
(Ecclesiastes 9:10; Philippians 2:13, KJV)

Y OO-HOO! Yoo-hoo! You women of Uganda, come over here!" The caller was Mama Ya Adija, an Indian woman who lived in Uganda, Africa. She was staying for a while in Zaire to get medical help from a missionary. Eight women, who had come to a market in Zaire to shop, squeezed through the crowds to hear what Mama Ya Adija had to say to them.

She held up her New Testament, saying, "You are Indians, just like me. I think, too, that you are just as I was when I came here—sad and hopeless, with nothing much to live for. But I've learned something wonderful that's in this Book. Listen to the words I have learned." Then she repeated one verse after another, until she had quoted 15 verses.

A missionary had been teaching Mama Ya Adija to read. As soon as she had memorized just 15 verses, the poor, sick lady went to the market to witness to others. What happened? The eight women wanted to be saved, and a Christian man led them to Jesus. Mama Ya Adija worked for God, using the little that she knew. In this Bible story, another woman served God with what she had—a bottle of milk and a tent peg.

The Facts, Please!

1. Since early Old Testament days, people used sweet milk, which they obtained from cows, sheep, goats, and camels. Since there was no refrigeration, sweet milk had to be used quickly. Sour milk was used in a curdled form similar to yogurt, which could be kept longer. Often it was mixed with meat and dried. Later, water would be added to make a refreshing drink. This was what the woman in our story gave the sleepy general when he asked for a drink of water.

2. In Palestine, tents were used by nomadic people, shepherds, and soldiers. The tents were often made of a long piece of cloth that was woven from black goat's hair. The cloth was stretched over a series of poles, and the two ends were pinned to the ground

with tent pegs. The side and end walls were made of reed mats, colored materials, or worn roof coverings. These could be lifted up to let in a breeze.

Bible Story: The General's Fatal Sleep
(Judges 4)

The Israelites were in great trouble. Because they had begun to worship idols, God allowed King Jabin from a northern country to invade their land. His army, led by General Sisera, rode across the countryside in nine hundred chariots of iron—stealing, burning villages, and enslaving the people. After suffering for 20 years, the Israelites asked God to forgive them and help them drive Sisera's army away.

At that time a woman judge named Deborah sat under a palm tree, giving advice to people who had problems. One day Deborah called for a soldier named Barak and said, "God says you must gather an army of 10,000 soldiers and fight against General Sisera and his army. God will help you defeat them."

Barak answered, "I won't go, unless you go with me."

"I will go," the brave woman replied, "but you won't get the glory for winning. A woman will conquer Sisera."

Barak and Deborah led the Israelite soldiers to Mount Tabor. General Sisera brought his big army, with its nine hundred iron chariots, to a river near the foot of the mountain. Then the Israelites, with swords, charged down the hill toward them. God sent a rainstorm that flooded the river and caused the chariots of Sisera's army to be mired in the mud. Barak and his men fought and destroyed them all—all except Sisera.

When the general saw that his army was defeated, he leaped out of his chariot and ran away on foot. Soon he came to a tent, where a woman named Jael invited him in. "I'm thirsty," said Sisera. "May I have some water?" Jael gave him some curdled milk in a large bowl. After he drank it, she covered him with a mantle, and the exhausted general fell asleep.

Jael took a tent peg and a mallet in her hand. Softly, she sneaked up to Sisera, placed the sharp peg on his temple, and pounded it hard, pinning him to the ground. When Barak, who was pursuing Sisera, came up, Jael said, "Come in. Here is the man you are looking for." Sure enough, there lay Sisera, dead by the hand of a woman, just as Deborah had said.

This Is for You

When there is work to be done for the Lord, he is the one who helps us and gives the victory. Our part is to yield to him and let him use whatever we have and are. Mama Ya Adija used her little Bible knowledge to win eight souls to Jesus. Jael used very simple things—some milk and a tent peg—to help God's people defeat their enemy.

Do we think we don't have much to serve Jesus? We have a brain; we can use it to study and memorize God's Word. We have a tongue; we can use it to be witnesses for God. We have hands and feet; we can use them to serve and help others. We don't have to wait until we're grown. Let's get busy with what we have right now!

What Can You Do for Jesus?

God gives each person talents and abilities that they can use to work for him. He says, "Whatever your hand finds to do, do it with all your might" (Ecclesiastes 9:10). This doesn't mean your hands only, but any part of your body and any talents you have.

On a separate sheet of paper trace the outline of your hand. Then on each finger write one thing that you can do for Jesus. Sign your name below the hand if you will try to do those things.

27

Shipwreck!

Introduction

"Last night an angel of the God whose I am and whom I serve stood beside me and said, 'Do not be afraid, Paul. . . . God has graciously given you the lives of all who sail with you.' So keep up your courage, men, for I have faith in God that it will happen just as he told me."

(Acts 27:23-25)

HAVE you ever been in serious danger? Did you do your best to take care of yourself? Perhaps the situation was so bad that you couldn't do anything. If so, did you call on God to help you? The apostle Paul and 275 other people were in a very dangerous situation one time. Paul knew that there was no help from anyone but God. He was a prisoner sailing on a ship in a monstrous, violent storm.

The Facts, Please!

1. Because boats in ancient days were not very sturdy, sailing was always dangerous. At first, the sailing was done only on rivers. Finally, some sailors ventured into the Persian Gulf and the Mediterranean Sea. The Phoenicians were the first to develop trade along the shores of the Mediterranean. In Greek and Roman times, larger and better vessels were built, and shipping was extended even farther.

2. Early boats were made of fir, pine, or cedar boards over a hardwood frame. Ropes, cables, or chains (called "helps" in the King James Version) were usually kept on board to strengthen the hull in a storm. They were passed around the hull and tightened with wooden levers.

3. The ship on which Paul sailed was a cargo vessel that carried grain. It had a huge mast with a large, square sail. There was a small sail, called a "foresail," that could be hoisted instead of the larger one in stormy weather. Four anchors were carried on the stern (the rear end), and two or more were on the prow (the front end). A small rowboat, for use when the ship was in harbor, was towed behind the big ship. In a storm it was kept on board. Navigation (plotting the ship's course) was done by looking at the position of the sun or stars.

4. The weather was too dangerous for sailing from November until March. Roman law forbade sailing

then unless there was an emergency or a trader was willing to take a chance.

Bible Story: Abandon Ship!
(Acts 27)

A ferocious wind howled out of the northeast over the Mediterranean Sea, tossing the ship around like a toy. Huge waves slammed against the ship, and spray whipped across its deck. The sky grew black with clouds, lit up only by streaks of lightning. Sheets of rain poured down. On board, the 276 passengers and sailors feared for their lives.

Earlier, the ship had been harbored at Fair Havens to escape another storm. When the south wind blew softly, the captain decided to sail on to a better port to spend the winter.

A very important passenger was on that ship—the apostle Paul, who was being taken to Rome as a prisoner for preaching about Jesus. "We should spend the winter here," Paul had advised. "If we don't, there will be much hurt and damage to the ship and to all of us." But the captain had sailed anyway. Now the ship and all on board were in terrible trouble. "Furl the mainsail!" ordered the captain. The men at the rudders gave up trying to steer the ship and let it run before the gale. Over and over again it rose up on the crest of a huge wave and dropped down into its trough with a *thud*. The sailors uncoiled cables and wrapped them around the hull to keep the ship from falling apart. They threw their cargo of grain and the ship's tackle overboard.

The storm raged for two weeks, with neither the sun nor the stars shining. They were completely lost at sea. Paul said, "If you had listened to me, this harm wouldn't have come to you. But be of good cheer. An angel of God told me last night that no one on this ship will be lost."

One night they heard the surf crashing against rocks. *Rocks!* They'd be dashed to pieces! The sailors threw out four anchors and prayed for daylight. When it came, they saw an island and set sail for its shore. So far, so good—until the ship was tossed about in crosscurrents. The bow ran aground on a sandbar and wouldn't budge. The winds and wild waves whipped the stern until the doomed ship broke into pieces.

Everyone leaped into the sea and swam to shore or floated in on broken pieces of the ship. Were they all safe? They counted to see. Yes! All 276 people stood on the shore of the tiny island—just as God had promised!

This Is for You

Our lives are like vessels at sea, sometimes sailing smoothly, blown along by soft breezes, and at other times plowing through rough, stormy waters. Life isn't always easy; the going can get tough and dangerous. When it does, did you know that God can send his angels to protect us, wherever we are? One came to cheer Paul and to give him God's promise of his help. Why? Because Paul was God's child and was serving him. If we belong to God, he will send his angels to help us. Be of good cheer!

Match-Up:
How Well Do You Know Ships?

The story of Paul's shipwreck in Acts 27 is one of the most complete accounts of a sea voyage from ancient times. It's fascinating! And knowing about ships will help you understand it. Draw a line from each term to its meaning.

stern	a ship that carries freight
prow (bow)	the frame of a ship
mainsail	movable paddles for steering a ship
foresail	the large, principal sail
hull	the front of a ship
mast	plotting a ship's course
rudders	the back of a ship
anchor	a small, auxiliary sail
"helps" (KJV)	tall spar, rising vertically from a ship's deck
cargo vessel	ropes or chains tied around a ship's hull in a storm
navigation	a weight to keep a ship from drifting

Fishing for Money

Introduction

"So don't be a stumbling block to anyone, whether they are Jews or Gentiles or Christians. That is the plan I follow, too. I try to please everyone in everything I do, not doing what I like or what is best for me but what is best for them, so that they may be saved"

(1 Corinthians 10:32-33, TLB).

SUPPOSE you are playing with your friend, and his (or her) mother tells him (or her), "Go clean your room right now." Your friend begs you to help so there will be time to play afterwards. You have your parents' permission to go and play with another friend if you wish. Would you help your friend clean the room, or would you go and play elsewhere?

Sometimes there is no rule or law saying you must do a

certain thing, but you must make a decision based on whether you will please yourself or others. Jesus taught Peter a lesson about this when he told him to go fishing for tax money.

The Facts, Please!

1. When Jesus was on earth, the Roman Empire, which ruled over the Jews, made them pay income and property taxes, plus taxes on almost everything they did or bought. Besides that, there were religious taxes. Peter went fishing for money to pay a religious due—the temple tax.

2. Jewish law said that each Jew had to pay a half-shekel for the temple tax. A silver coin, the four-drachma, equaled a shekel in Jesus' day. It paid the tax for two people.

3. There is a fish in Palestine called the St. Peter's fish. It is also called the tilapa. These strange fish carry their eggs in their mouths. Later, their young fish live there. Even when the little fish go in search of food, they return to the mother's mouth. When a mother wants to keep her young ones out of her mouth, she picks up an object and holds it. A bright object, like a coin, especially attracts her.

4. Although Palestinian fishermen usually caught fish with a net, Jesus told Peter to throw in a hook and line, because only one fish was needed.

BiblE StoRy: PETER'S StRANqE CATcH
(MATTHEW 17:24-27)

One day, when Jesus and his disciples were in Capernaum, the temple tax collectors asked Peter, "Doesn't your master pay the temple tax?"

"Yes, he does," answered Peter.

Later, inside a house, Jesus asked Peter, "What do you think, Simon Peter? From whom do kings collect dues and taxes—from their own children or from conquered foreigners?"

"From foreigners," answered Peter.

"You are right," said Jesus. "That means, then, that the king's own children are free from paying taxes." Peter knew that Jesus was the Son of God. That meant he was the King of the universe. A king doesn't have to pay taxes. "To keep from offending the tax collectors," Jesus continued, "go to the lake. Throw in a line, and look in the mouth of the first fish you catch. You will find a four-drachma. Give it to the collectors to pay the temple tax for you and me."

Peter went to the Sea of Galilee and threw in his line. Soon a fish struck, and he hauled it in. It was probably a tilapa; and, sure enough, inside its mouth was the silver coin! Peter hurried to the collectors and paid the temple tax.

This Is foR You

Those tax collectors didn't believe that Jesus was the Son of God and the King of the universe. They thought he was just an ordinary man. If he had not paid the temple tax, they would have said, "That man Jesus tells people how to live, but he doesn't even obey our laws about paying religious dues." Jesus did something he didn't have to do so those people could find no blame in him.

As Christians, we are surely trying to obey God's commandments, the laws of the country, and the rules of our parents. Sometimes, though, we are given a choice that doesn't involve any laws or rules. We are free to do what we want. Then we must decide what is best for those around us. To be Christlike, we will want to please and help others more than ourselves. Then we will set a good example of Christian behavior and be witnesses to sinners.

Choose an Answer:
What Would You Do?

If the following situations happened to you, what would you do? Write your answer on the line that follows each situation.

1. The friend you are playing with must clean his (or her) room. You have permission to go and play with another friend. Would you stay and help your friend clean the room or go elsewhere to play? _____

2. You are visiting a crippled child, who asks you to stay and play a quiet game. Some of your friends ask you to play in a ball game. Which would you do?

   _____

3. You have been paid to rake the front yard belonging to an old lady. Her backyard needs raking, too, but she can't pay you to do both. Would you rake both yards or only the one? _____

4. It's your little sister's turn to do the dishes, but she wants to go to a birthday party and doesn't have time to wash dishes. Would you wash the dishes for her?

_____

5. You paid your tithe and gave an extra offering for missions. You are planning to buy a VCR tape with the rest of your money. The pastor takes up an offering for a family whose home burned up. Would you give them some money or buy the tape?

_____

Which of your answers could help you win a soul to Jesus or influence a new Christian to be Christlike? Write the numbers here: _____

The World's First Alarm Clock

Introduction

"Watch with me and pray lest the Tempter overpower you. For though the spirit is willing enough, the body is weak."

(Mark 14:38, TLB)

As two men sat in a boat, fishing in the middle of a lake, they heard a rooster crow. "That's strange," said one man. "I hear a rooster crowing, but we're nowhere near land, and besides, it's afternoon. Roosters don't usually crow then."

The other man smiled. "Mine does," he said. He pushed a little button on his wristwatch, and the crowing stopped. "The alarm on my watch is the sound of a rooster's crowing," he explained.

Do you like the sound of an alarm clock early in the morning? Probably not. Its jangling can be very disturbing when it wakes us from a sound sleep and we have to crawl out of a soft, warm bed to go to school. One night a rooster's alarm was very disturbing to Peter, one of Jesus' disciples.

The Facts, Please!

1. The first alarm clock invented by man, so far as we know, was a candle. Medieval monks slid a lighted candle between their toes when they took a nap. When the flame reached their skin, their "hot foot" woke them up! A New England clockmaker, Levi Hutchins, is credited with inventing the first clock with a bell that would wake a person at a set time.

2. The world's first alarm clock, though, was made by God. It was a rooster. Because a cock in the East crowed during the night at regular times, those times were called cockcrowing. Cockcrowing was used by the Romans when they divided the night into four watches (areas of time). They were: late, midnight, cockcrowing, and early. The Jews divided the night into three watches. Cockcrowing was at three o'clock in the morning.

3. A rooster crows by means of an organ called the syrinx. It is located where the windpipe splits into two bronchi (the tubes that carry air to his lungs).

Bible Story: Peter and the Rooster
(Matthew 26:31-35, 69-75)

The eleven disciples stopped dead in their tracks with their mouths open. What was that Jesus had just said? "Tonight you will all desert me." How could that be? Hadn't they followed him and worked with him for three years? They loved him dearly. Why, they would never, *never* leave him!

Peter spoke up. "If everyone else deserts you, I will never leave you!"

Jesus looked at Peter sadly. "This very night, before the cock crows, you will deny me three times."

"No! I will die before I deny you!" Peter declared. And all the other disciples said the same thing.

Jesus led the disciples out to the Garden of Gethsemane, where he prayed. Then, in the darkness there was a great commotion as Judas led soldiers to capture Jesus. He willingly went with them. But what about his brave disciples who said they'd never desert him? Scared to death, they all ran away.

The mob of Jews and soldiers took Jesus to the high priest's home to stand trial. John and Peter stopped running away and followed far behind. When they came to the high priest's house, John went inside, but Peter stayed out in the courtyard and warmed himself by a fire.

A servant girl came over and said to him, "You were with Jesus of Galilee."

Peter was terrified. Maybe he'd be captured, too! Maybe he'd be killed! Without stopping to think or ask God to help him, he said, "I don't know what you're talking about."

Soon another servant girl saw him. "This man was also with Jesus of Nazareth," she declared to those standing around.

"No, I was not!" Peter said, with an oath.

After a while, some others came to Peter and said, "Surely you are a disciple of Jesus, for you have a Galilean accent."

Oh, Peter was really frightened now! In his terror, he cursed and swore. "I do not know the man," he declared. Just then a rooster crowed. Peter looked through the door and saw Jesus looking at him. Then he remembered what Jesus had said: "Before the cock crows, you will deny me three times."

Alarm bells went off in Peter's head. He had not been faithful to Jesus, even to death, after all. He had denied him! He went out, away from everyone, and cried bitterly.

This Is for You

Was Peter a believer—a saved person? Yes, he was. He miserably failed and sinned, but he repented with bitter tears. Later, after rising from the dead, Jesus talked with Peter and forgave him. Then Peter served him faithfully.

How can we keep from stumbling into sin and failing Jesus? We can do what Jesus told the disciples to do: "Watch and pray, so you won't fall into temptation." Right after Jesus said that, he led the disciples into the Garden of Gethsemane. While he went alone to pray, he told them to pray, also. What did Peter and the others do? They fell asleep.

Here are some tips to help us say no to sin when we are tempted: Read our Bibles to know what is right and wrong. Pray, asking God to help us resist temptations. Try to stay away from places or people that we know could tempt us to sin. With God's help, we can have victory over sin.

Fill in the Blanks:
How to Keep from Failing Jesus

Here is a good formula that will help you stay true to Jesus, if you will follow it. To learn what it is, read the following Scriptures in your Bible and fill in the blanks.

PSALM 119:11: Hide (store) God's __ __ __ __ in your __ __ __ __ __ so you won't __ __ __.

LUKE 22:40: __ __ __ __ that you won't fall into temptation.

PROVERBS 1:8: __ __ __ __ __ __ __ to the teachings of your __ __ __ __ __ __ __ and __ __ __ __ __ __ __.

PROVERBS 4:14-15: Don't follow in the ways of the __ __ __ __ __ __.

EPHESIANS 6:11: Put on the full __ __ __ __ __ of God, so you can stand against the tricks of the __ __ __ __ __.

EPHESIANS 6:16: Use the shield of __ __ __ __ __.

30

The Dead Stick That Came Alive

Introduction

"Do not fear, for I am with you; do not be dismayed, for I am your God. I will strengthen you and help you; I will uphold you with my righteous right hand."

(Isaiah 41:10)

ONE time a missionary in Africa had to travel through a dark forest. He knew some men lived nearby who had threatened to kill him for preaching about Jesus. After asking God to protect him, the missionary made the trip. The next day, his enemies came to him and asked, "Who were those two giant men who walked on either side of you last night? We meant to ambush you and kill you, but we were afraid after seeing them."

"My God protected me with his angels," said the missionary. The Lord had helped the missionary by working a miracle. He had sent his angels to walk beside the missionary, and he caused his enemies to see them. Because of this, the missionary won the men to the Lord, and they became his good friends.

Moses had work to do for the Lord, but he was afraid he couldn't do it. God showed him he didn't have to do it alone; he would have God's power to help him. So that Moses would know he was there to help him, God brought a dead stick to life.

THE FACTS, PLEASE!

1. Moses' "dead stick" was a shepherd's walking staff. When he was 40 years old, Moses went out into the desert and became a sheepherder. That is where he first used his staff.

2. In Bible times, a shepherd's staff was from three to six feet long, usually with a crook at one end. This staff helped the shepherd climb hills or walk across the rough countryside. He used it to beat the bushes or brush when a sheep strayed into it. This helped him find the sheep and scare away any snakes or other reptiles that happened to be there.

3. The shepherd's rod was used to count the sheep. At night, when the sheep were brought into the sheepfold or herded together, they passed under the rod, one by one and were counted. It was used to mark the sheep. The end of a rod was dipped in dye, and every tenth sheep that passed under the rod was marked as a tithe and was later given to God in the temple.

Bible Story: The Rod of Many Miracles
(Exodus 4:1-5, 29-31; 7:8-21; 14:15-31; 17:1-7; Numbers 17:1-10)

One day as Moses watched his sheep in the desert, he saw a very strange thing, a bush that was on fire but didn't burn up. When he came closer, he heard God speaking. "Go back to Egypt and lead the Israelites out of their life of slavery and into the land I have given them."

"But the Israelites won't believe you have sent me to do this," Moses said. He had been out of Egypt for 40 years. Surely the Israelites wouldn't follow a desert shepherd!

"What is that in your hand?" God asked.

"A shepherd's rod," answered Moses. God told him to throw it on the ground. When he did, the rod turned into a serpent. Moses ran away, fast. His dead stick had become a living thing!

"Take hold of its tail," God commanded. Moses grabbed the tail, and the snake became a rod again. "Do this same thing before the Israelite leaders," God said.

Moses said he couldn't speak well, so God told him to take his brother, Aaron, to do the talking. When Moses performed the miracle with the rod, the Israelites promised to let him lead them.

Next, Moses and Aaron asked Pharaoh to let the Israelites go. They threw down the rod, and God turned it into a snake. When Pharaoh's magicians did the same thing (by some kind of trick or by demonic power), Moses' snake ate up their snakes.

More miracles were done with the rod. Aaron struck the Nile River with it, and all the waters in Egypt turned to blood. When Pharaoh finally let the Israelites leave Egypt, Moses stretched his rod over the Red Sea, and the waters rolled back to let more than two million Israelites pass through on dry land. Again, he stretched out his rod, and the waters came back in place, drowning the pursuing Egyptian soldiers.

As they journeyed into the desert, the Israelites had no water to drink. God told Moses to strike a rock with the rod. When he did, water poured out—enough for all the thirsty people. Another time, the rod budded and blossomed and had ripe almonds on it to show that Aaron was the high priest whom God had chosen. Again, the dead stick became a living thing!

This Is for You

Moses felt like a nobody. He was sure God couldn't use him. What Moses needed was some help. Through his simple shepherd's rod, he learned that the Lord was with him to work miracles and make him somebody that God could use.

Do we feel like nobodies? Are we afraid to try to witness for God or serve him in other ways? We have the same help that Moses did. We have Almighty God. Just as Moses held onto his rod, we can hold onto God's Word and the promises he has written in it. God wants us to trust him and not to be afraid to work for him. He will be with us to help us and take care of us. To him, we are *special people* he can use, if we will trust him and not be afraid.

Find the Missing Letters:
Never Fear—God Is Here

If God asks you to do something for him, he will be near to help you and take care of you. Write the letter that's missing from the second word in each sentence on the line with the matching number. The letters will spell what God thinks about you and what he can do with you.

1. In MAST but not in MAT.
2. In PLUCK but not in LUCK.
3. In GAPE but not in GAP.
4. In CLOCK but not in LOCK.
5. In MAID but not in MAD.
6. In COAT but not in COT.
7. In BLOW but not in BOW.
8. In PAIN but not in PIN.
9. In RAFT but no in RAT.
10. In FRAME but not in FAME.
11. In SPAIN but not in SPIN.
12. In RAIN but not in RAN.
13. In TEND but not in TEN.

To God, you are somebody __ __ __ __ __ __ __.
$\qquad\qquad\qquad\qquad$ 1 2 3 4 5 6 7

God can use you if you will trust him and not be

__ __ __ __ __ __.
8 9 10 11 12 13

31

Marching Orders

Introduction

"Listen, I tell you a mystery: We will not all sleep, but we will all be changed—in a flash, in the twinkling of an eye, at the last trumpet. For the trumpet will sound, the dead will be raised imperishable, and we will be changed."

(1 Corinthians 15:51-52)

It's early in the morning, and you're at school, perhaps in a hallway or near your locker. A bell rings or a buzzer sounds. You hurry to your classroom because you know that school is about to start. After a while, a bell or buzzer sounds again, and you march to your next class. There are signals for recess or lunchtime, and there is the last bell or buzzer (perhaps your favorite) that lets you know school is out for the

181

day. Do you respond to those signals at once? Are you sometimes tardy?

In Bible times marching orders were given by trumpet blasts. Someday all Christians will receive special "marching orders," when we hear what the Bible calls "the last trumpet." No one can be tardy then. If you're not ready, you won't go.

The Facts, Please!

1. Trumpets, also called horns or cornets, are mentioned in several places in the Bible. They were made of either metal or bone. Their sounding air column was about two feet long. This produced a high, shrill tone.

2. The bone trumpets were usually made from a ram's horn. The Jews called this a shofar. It was used to signal a battle or peace at the end of a battle, the beginning of the Sabbath, the first day of the month, and the Year of Jubilee. In the month of Tishri they blew these trumpets all day long on the first day of the Festival of Trumpets.

3. When God gave Moses instructions for building the tabernacle, he also commanded that two silver trumpets should be made. These were to be blown as signals to the Israelites when they were camped in the wilderness. One long blast by the two trumpets meant that all the people were to assemble before Moses at the door of the tabernacle. If the long blast was blown on only one trumpet, just the tribal lead-

ers were to assemble. A special blast, called an "alarm," was sounded when the camps were to march forward.

4. Paul said that when Jesus came in the air to take us to heaven, the "last trumpet" would sound. The people in Palestine in those days were familiar with Roman soldiers, who were signalled by three trumpet calls. The first blast meant "Strike tents and be ready to depart." The second meant "Fall into line." The last trumpet meant "March!"

BiblE Story: THE TRUMPET CAll TO MARCH
(NUMBERS 10:1-36)

For about a year the children of Israel camped beneath Mount Sinai, where God gave them the Ten Commandments and other laws. They built the tabernacle according to his directions. God stayed above it, showing his presence by a pillar of cloud in the daytime and a pillar of fire at night.

One morning the people stepped out of their tents as usual. "Look!" someone called out. "The pillar of cloud is moving!" Everyone knew what that meant—it was time for them to move, too. Mothers called for their children to come in from play. Families worked together to pack their belongings and take down their tents. The priests took down the tabernacle.

When all was ready, they lined up by tribe, with each tribe's banner flying overhead. Then two priests blew an alarm with a blast on their silver trumpets. The camp on the east side of the tabernacle marched forward. As other alarms sounded, the remaining tribes marched. They knew just where to go because the cloud moved ahead of them.

After three days' journey, the cloud stopped. The Israelites stopped, too, and set up camp. They stayed at that place until the day when the trumpets sounded the special alarm again, and they began to march once more.

This Is for You

One day, maybe very soon, there will be a long blast from a trumpet that will be heard around the world by God's children. It will be God's trumpet, sounding from the skies—probably the most beautiful music ever heard. It will be our marching orders for glory. All believers who have died will hear it. Their dead bodies will rise, changed to perfect new bodies. When the living believers hear it, they will receive their new bodies. Together we will go up to meet the Lord in the air. Immediately, we'll be with him in heaven. It won't be a slow march. It will happen faster than an eye can blink.

Like the Roman soldiers of long ago, we have three trumpet blasts from God. The first one is his call for us to repent of sins and trust Jesus as Savior—to "prepare to meet your God." If we answer and obey the first trumpet call, our second call is to fall in line with God's people as soldiers of the Cross and serve him, the Commander-in-Chief. We will only hear God's last trumpet if we have answered his first call to trust Jesus. Get prepared now! Our marching orders will come without any warning. Don't be left behind!

Fill the Blanks:
A Christian's Three Trumpet Calls

Christians hear three calls, but the words to the calls here are mixed up. Beginning with the first call, write the first word in the sentence below in the first blank and then write each third word after that. Do the same with the second call, using the second word from the beginning of the sentence and each third word after that; and then finally the third call, using the third word from the beginning of the sentence and each third word after that. You may want to number the words before you write them in so you don't get the calls mixed up.

Believe Thou And on therefore behold the endure I Lord hardness come Jesus as quickly Christ a and and good my thou soldier reward shalt of is be Jesus with saved Christ me.

First Trumpet Call: "_____ _____ _____ _____

_____ _____, _____ _____ _____ _____

_____" (Acts 16:31).

Second Trumpet Call: "_____ _____ _____

_____, _____ _____ _____ _____ _____

_____ _____" (2 Timothy 2:3).

Third Trumpet Call: "_____, _____, _____

_____ _____; _____ _____ _____ _____

_____ _____" (Revelation 22:12).

32

Fig Leaves, Furs, Filthy Rags, and Fine Linen

Introduction

"All our righteousnesses are as filthy rags. . . . [God] hath clothed me with the garments of salvation, he hath covered me with the robe of righteousness."

(Isaiah 64:6; 61:10, KJV)

A boy walks down the street with jeans that have large, ragged holes in the knees, a T-shirt that is much too big, shoes that light up when he steps, a cap that is on backwards, and an earring in one ear. He considers himself to be wearing the latest style for boys. But in a year or two, he probably won't wear the outfit for a million bucks, because it will be out of style and something else will be the rage.

Do you like to wear the latest styles, at least if they're not too outrageous? Once everybody in the world wore fig leaves. After that, furs were the fashion. The Bible talks of clothing styles, too—spiritual clothing. It says this clothing can be either filthy rags or fine, white linen.

The Facts, Please!

1. Fig leaves—These were the "in" fashion for a while, since they were worn by all people in the world at the time—Adam and Eve. The leaves were large with deep lobes, and they sewed the leaves together to make coverings. There are over a hundred different kinds of fig trees, most of them growing in countries around the Mediterranean Sea.

2. Furs—Since fig leaves didn't cover well and withered quickly, Adam and Eve needed something else to wear. God gave them furs—the skins of animals. In order for these to be worn, an animal had to be killed and its blood shed. Who killed it? We don't know. Maybe God did, or he taught Adam how to do it.

3. Filthy rags—Some people consider themselves to be "in style" spiritually because of their own good deeds, even if they don't believe in Jesus. They think they have on robes of righteousness, but God sees them wearing very dirty, bad-smelling rags.

4. Fine linen—In heaven, fine linen is the "in" thing for the bride of Christ (the church) to wear at her wedding feast. God offers this garment of salvation—

a pure white robe of Christ's righteousness—to any who will repent of sin and believe in Jesus as Savior. He bought these robes with his blood when he died on the cross.

Bible Story: Clothed in the Latest Styles
(Genesis 3:6-21; Revelation 19:8)

"Gimme some skin!" Have you ever heard that expression? The person speaking is really saying, "Shake hands with me." One day Adam and Eve needed some skin—clothes of skin, that is. But that's getting ahead of the story.

It was a sad, awful day in the Garden of Eden. Eve had just listened to the serpent and had eaten the forbidden fruit. She gave some to Adam, and he ate it, too. Then, because the fruit was from the tree of knowledge of good and evil, their eyes were opened and they realized they were naked.

"We must cover ourselves," Adam said to Eve. They picked some branches from the fig tree and laced them together at the waist so that the fig leaves covered them a little bit. But they still felt ashamed and naked. "God will soon come to talk with us. Let's hide behind those trees!" exclaimed Adam.

God saw them sin. He saw their nakedness and their poor attempt to cover it up. After he talked with them about their sin and told them about their great punishment, he gave them coats of skin to wear. Their fur coats came from an animal that had been killed and its blood shed. At this time, God must have taught Adam and Eve that they needed to kill an animal and shed its blood for a sin offering.

This was a picture of what Jesus was going to do someday. He died for the sins of the whole world, and he shed his blood to wash away sins. Now he offers a garment of salvation to any person who will believe on him.

This Is for You

All of us are born naked—not just in our bodies, but spiritually. We are born sinners, and we have all sinned. God sees our nakedness, and he offers to cover us up with a garment of salvation. Jesus bought that by dying on the cross and shedding his blood. God will only give us our pure white robe of Christ's righteousness when we trust Jesus as Savior.

What kind of spiritual clothes are we wearing right now? Do we have on filthy rags because we are trusting in our own good works? Or do we have on God's garment of salvation? If we do, we will wear fine, white linen robes and go to heaven someday and be a part of the bride of Christ at the wonderful wedding feast. God offers us these garments. It's up to us to be "in style."

Match-up:
Descriptions of Clothing

Below is a list of the clothing styles mentioned in this lesson. Match each one with its proper description.

Fig leaves	Spiritual clothing given to anyone who repents of sin and trusts Christ as Savior
Furs	Clothing worn by people who trust in their good deeds for their salvation, not in Jesus
Filthy rags	Aprons made by Adam and Eve to try to cover themselves
Garment of salvation	Robes worn at the wedding feast in heaven by the bride of Christ
Robe of righteousness	Coats made by God for Adam and Eve to wear
Fine linen, clean and white	Another name for the garment of salvation—made, not of our own goodness, but of Christ's

33

A Tiny Ant
and a Big Lesson

Introduction

"Yet we hear that some of you are living in laziness, refusing to work, and wasting your time in gossiping. In the name of the Lord Jesus Christ we appeal to such people—we command them—to quiet down, get to work, and earn their own living. And to the rest of you I say, dear brothers, never be tired of doing right."

(2 Thessalonians 3:11-13, TLB)

Do any of these speeches sound familiar? "Turn off the TV and do your homework." "Stop talking on the phone so much and clean your messy room." "Get up, lazybones! Are you going to sleep all day?" "Come in the house! It's your turn to do the dishes." When your parents say things like that, are they just picking on you? No, for your own future

193

good, they are trying to teach you not to be lazy and to be a good worker. God doesn't want us to be lazy, either. In the book of Proverbs he uses the tiny ant to teach us about being industrious and hardworking.

The Facts, Please!

1. There are eight thousand known species of ants that live on all the earth's land surfaces except the polar regions. The world's ant population is 10 million billion—more than all mammals, birds, reptiles, and amphibians combined!

2. Ants live together in large colonies, some of which contain millions of ants. The ants in the nest help one another, sharing both their food and their work. Each colony contains at least one queen, male ants, and workers. All of these are extremely important for the life of the colony.

   The queens lay most of the eggs. Sometimes there is one queen to a colony; other times there are several. The only work of the male ants is to mate with the queen ants. Most ants in the colony are worker ants. The worker ants are females who usually cannot lay eggs. The queen ant is bigger than the workers. In some species, she is more than one thousand times as big!

   Worker ants collect the food, feed the young ants, build the nest, and take care of all the needs of the queen. There are soldier ants, who protect the nest, and nurse ants, who care for the young.

3. Some ants can lift things that weigh 50 times their own weight. That's equivalent to a person lifting 10,000 pounds! Compared to the size of the builders, their large mounds are three times larger than the Egyptian pyramids.

4. The ants that are spoken of in Proverbs are the harvester ants. They eat seeds. In the Holy Land, they often nest near where grain is thrashed or stored and carry it into storehouses in their nests. When winter comes, they have plenty to eat.

Bible Story: Lazy Person, Look at the Ant
(Proverbs 6:6-11; 30:25)

Lazy fellow, get up out of bed and go look at an ant nest. The ants have a lesson to teach you. See what they are doing. They take care of themselves. They work hard to provide for the needs of all the ants in their colony.

They don't have a commander, an overseer, or a ruler to tell them what to do. They get right to work, doing whatever job needs to be done.

They work all through the hot days of summer, storing up large quantities of seeds for the winter months. In some nests there may be a bushel of seeds stored up. They and their little ones won't starve in the cold weather. There is plenty for all because they planned and prepared for the time when there would be no seeds or grains.

What do you do, lazy fellow? You sleep. You say, "Let me sleep a little longer! Let me fold my hands and rest."

And while you sleep and rest and do nothing, poverty will sneak up on you like a robber, and you will have no way to fight against it.

This Is for You

When we're young, our lives as grown-ups seem very far away. We'd rather think only of today or of the near future than to be concerned with a distant time. God wants us to copy the ants. They work for the future. Does that mean he doesn't ever want us to have a good time or "goof off"? Not at all! Fun, games, and recreational activities are all a part of learning, too. And they are necessary in order to take good care of our health.

How can we prepare for our future instead of being lazy? One way is to study our school lessons to the best of our ability. Another way is to develop our talents—like taking music lessons and practicing faithfully, or attending art or craft classes— and doing our best at whatever we do. We can discipline ourselves to keep a clean room, to take care of our clothes, and to save our money. Best of all, we can read and study God's Word, memorizing as much as we can.

Our youthful days will be gone before we know it. Like the industrious ant, let's prepare for our future days while we can. When we're grown, we'll thank our younger selves for providing for that time so well, and God will be well pleased, too.

Your Resolutions:
Preparing for Your Future

What are you doing now to prepare for a good future that will please God? In what ways can you be more hardworking and industrious right now? (You may want some help for this from a parent.) Write your answers on the lines below.

I am already preparing for my future life by: _____

_____

_____

I need to improve in these areas of my life: _____

_____

_____

I'd like to start doing these things: _____

_____

_____

With God's help, I will try to be like the ant—working hard and preparing for the future.

Signed: _____

Frogs in Pharaoh's Bed

Introduction

"Ah Lord God! behold, thou hast made the heaven and the earth by thy great power and stretched out arm, and there is nothing too hard for thee."

(Jeremiah 32:17, KJV)

If you had $1,000 in the bank, would you be worried if you needed a new pair of shoes? No. You'd write out a check and buy the shoes. But what if you needed something that cost a million dollars? Would your bank account cover that need? No way! If a billionaire gave you a blank check with his signature, though, you could have your need met.

There are many things that you can't do for yourself, and even a billionaire has limits to what he can do. But you have a Friend who can do anything he wants to do and who has unlimited riches—God. He has performed many miracles to prove that he is all-powerful. One of these was the miracle of the frogs.

THE FACTS, PLEASE!

1. There are more than two thousand different kinds of frogs in the world today. Since they are amphibians, they are able to live on land and in the water. Some frogs, though, never come on land but spend their whole lives in the water. Others always live on land and never in water. Some frogs even live in trees.

2. Frogs are cold-blooded animals, and many of them hibernate in the winter. In the spring, they leave their holes and go to some water, where the female lays eggs and the male fertilizes them. The eggs are covered with a kind of jellied substance to protect them. Then, after 4 to 15 days, they hatch into tadpoles. In a few months (or as much as two years for a bullfrog), the tadpole's tail has been absorbed, and it has grown legs and lungs. It has become a frog.

3. In Egypt there are frogs that live in water and on land. In July, when the Nile River overflows and then recedes, it leaves many stagnant pools of water. In August and September, the frogs breed in the pools. In the days of the Pharaohs, hordes of frogs coming out of these pools were common. But the plague of frogs that God sent upon them was different and much worse.

4. The Egyptians considered frogs sacred, and they worshiped a female god that had a frog's head. It was very upsetting and humiliating to them when frogs invaded their land and caused them a very revolting problem.

Bible Story: The Revolting Frog Invasion
(Exodus 8:1-15; Psalm 105:30)

"Let my people go that they may hold a feast to me in the wilderness," God told Pharaoh through his messenger, Moses. But Pharaoh refused to obey God, so Aaron stretched his rod over the waters in Egypt, and they turned to blood. Still Pharaoh wouldn't let the Israelites leave.

"You'd better obey God," Moses told Pharaoh. "If you don't, God will fill your land with frogs."

Pharaoh snorted. "So what? Frogs always come out at this time of year. Anyhow, frogs are very sacred to us. We worship them. Let the frogs come! But you are not going anywhere!"

Aaron stretched out his rod over the streams, rivers, and ponds. Immediately, great hordes of frogs covered the land. They hopped into the small, mud-brick houses of the poorest people; they climbed over the walls that surrounded the homes of the rich and invaded every corner of their palatial dwellings.

People scrunched frogs under their feet wherever they stepped. In order to sit down, they had to shoo away the frogs. When the women got out their kneading bowls to make bread, they found frogs sitting in their dough; and the creatures were even in their ovens.

The frogs overran Pharaoh's palace. He pulled back the covers of his bed to go to sleep, and out they hopped. His servants shook out the frogs, but when Pharaoh climbed into bed, they crawled over his face.

Pharaoh's magicians also produced some frogs—not, of course, by creating them instantly as God did. Maybe they secretly put some inside their clothes and pulled them out by a sleight-of-hand trick. They could do nothing to make all the frogs go away, though.

Finally Pharaoh called for Moses and begged him to ask God to get rid of the frogs. "Then you may leave," he promised. "Get rid of the frogs tomorrow." Moses and Aaron prayed, and the next day every frog died except those in the river. There were dead frogs all over the place. People gathered them in great heaps, and they smelled awful! Had Pharaoh learned his lesson? No. Again he refused to let the Israelites go.

This Is for You

Pharaoh, the ruler of all Egypt, could do nothing about the frogs, and his magicians couldn't get rid of them. It was nothing for God to produce hordes of frogs. And it was just as easy to get rid of them. There is nothing too hard for him.

We should remember this when our problems seem to pop up all around us like the frogs that covered Egypt. If we think there's no way out, we can look up to our heavenly Father, who is able to take care of any situation. There is only one limit to what he will do—he won't sin or do something that is not for our good. Let's pray for him to meet our needs according to his will, believe him, and wait for him to answer. He can do it!

Unscramble Words and Fill Blanks:
What Can God Do?

Some people doubt that God can do anything he wants to do. Fill the words in the sentence about God on the next page by first unscrambling some words taken from the story of the miracle of the frogs. Then place the numbered letters in their proper spaces.

HAROAPH __ __ __ __ __ __ __
$\qquad\quad$ 3

SEMOS __ __ __ __ __
$\qquad\;$ 5

RANOA __ __ __ __ __
$\qquad\quad$ 12 $\quad$ 14

ODG __ __ __
$\quad$ 1

GSORF __ __ __ __ __
$\qquad\;$ 6

NEVO __ __ __ __
$\qquad$ 2 $\quad$ 7

DEB __ __ __
$\qquad$ 10

GUDOH __ __ __ __ __
$\qquad\quad$ 4 8

MASSTRE __ __ __ __ __ __ __
$\qquad\;$ 9

VERISR __ __ __ __ __ __
$\qquad\;$ 11

TEEF __ __ __ __
$\qquad\;$ 13

God can do everything, because there is

$$\overline{7}\ \overline{1}\ \overline{9}\ \overline{3}\ \overline{11}\ \overline{14}\ \overline{4}\quad \overline{13}\ \overline{5}\ \overline{2}\quad \overline{8}\ \overline{12}\ \overline{6}\ \overline{10}$$ for him.

35

Sun and Moon, Stand Still!

Introduction

"How we thank God for all of this! It is he who makes us victorious through Jesus Christ our Lord!"

(1 Corinthians 15:57, TLB)

ONE time a little girl and her brother were looking at a sunset. "Look! The sun is sinking down!" said the girl.

"Don't be silly," said her brother. "The sun doesn't move. The earth is moving. It is turning away from the sun."

"No, you're wrong," insisted the little girl. "I'm standing on the earth, and I'm not moving. But the sun is. I can see it going down more and more and . . . *there!* It's gone!"

Of course, you know the little girl was wrong. But it does really seem to us that the earth is standing still and the sun is moving. God made the earth and the sun to work exactly right in relation to each other, so that human beings, plants, and animals could exist on earth. One time, however, he changed all that when the sun shone in the sky for almost 24 hours.

The Facts, Please!

1. God created the sun and the moon to make day and night on earth and to divide our seasons and years. Without them, every living thing would die.

2. The solar system is made up of the sun, the planets, and all the other heavenly bodies—such as moons, asteroids, and many meteors. The planets and smaller bodies are held in place by the pull of the sun, as they travel around it and receive and reflect its light and heat. Each has a regular path (orbit) around the sun.

3. The diameter of the sun is 865,400 miles, which is 109 times the diameter of the earth and 400 times the diameter of the moon. If the sun were a two-foot ball, the earth would be the size of a pea. The earth makes one revolution around the sun in a year's time. At the same time, it spins once around its axis daily, giving us light (day) and darkness (night).

4. Our solar system is a small part of a galaxy, called the Milky Way, which consists of 100 billion stars. Some are 10 miles in diameter; some are as big as 330 times the size of our sun. Today's telescopes can identify more than one billion galaxies in the universe.

5. If God can make this huge universe and keep it all running in place and in order, he can also change any part of it if he chooses to do so. The Bible tells an incredible story about a day when he did that—the day the sun stood still. How did this come about? Did God stop the rotation of the earth, so that the sun appeared to stand still? Did he cause the whole solar system to stop in place for a day? It doesn't matter how it happened, but we know it did because the Bible says so.

Bible Story: The Longest Day
(Joshua 10:1-43)

When the Israelites marched into Canaan, they began to fight against the wicked idol worshipers who lived there, just as God had told them to do. Under their leader, Joshua, they destroyed city after city.

One day, perhaps as Joshua sat planning his next campaign, some men from Gibeon rushed in to where he was. "Come quickly with your army to save us!" they begged. "Five kings and their armies have surrounded our city and are fighting against us."

Joshua had made a treaty with Gibeon, so he gathered his soldiers together at once. "Don't be afraid of those kings and their men," God told him, "for I have given them to you to destroy. None of them will be able to stand against you."

All night Joshua and his men marched toward Gibeon. Early in the morning, they sneaked up on the sleeping armies and attacked them. The surprised soldiers panicked

and ran, with Joshua's men pursuing them and killing a
great many. Suddenly, the sky grew black, and great hailstones fell on the fleeing army. They killed more men than
Joshua's army had done. Still, some escaped, and the day
was ending. Joshua knew he must finish the fight before
nightfall, or they would reach their own cities and return to
fight later. He needed more daylight!

Joshua prayed to the Lord. Then in a loud voice he cried,
"Sun, stand still! Moon, remain where you are!" Did God
actually stop the sun and the moon to answer one man's
prayer? Yes! The daylight continued for almost 24 hours,
until Joshua's forces had destroyed the enemy. There has
never been a day like that before nor since.

This Is for You

"Fight the enemy armies, and I will give you the
victory," God told Joshua. He obeyed. To help him, God
sent hailstones and kept the sun shining for almost 24
hours.

Are there some things we need to get the victory over?
Maybe our tongue gets us in trouble because we speak
before we think. Maybe we're very shy and are afraid to
stand up for what's right when we're with our schoolmates.
Maybe we quarrel and fight with our brothers and sisters or
talk back to our parents. Maybe we want to do something
special for the Lord, but someone or something stands in
our way.

Whatever our needs are, we can have the victory if we'll
let Jesus control us and fight our battles beside us. He will

allow nothing to stop us when we are ready to follow his orders and trust him to give us the victory.

Verse Maze:
With God on Our Side

No one can defeat God. Do you have friends or family members who oppose you in your Christian life? Are temptations, sinners, or Satan making it difficult for you to do right? Romans 8:31 (KJV) says, "If God be for us, who can be against us?" With a pencil, trace these words, in order, through the maze five times, going up, down, right, and left.

D	O	I	S	W	C	A	E	A	I	N	S
B	G	F	U	H	O	N	B	G	A	U	T
E	F	O	R	U	R	O	F	D	O	S	?
I	A	E	B	S	W	H	E	B	G	F	I
N	G	A	N	A	C	O	O	D	F	O	R
S	T	U	S	?	I	F	G	B	E	S	U
I	?	S	U	T	S	A	G	B	N	W	H
F	D	B	O	R	N	I	A	E	A	C	O
G	O	E	F	U	S	W	C	A	E	A	G
N	A	H	W	R	O	H	O	N	B	I	A
B	C	O	S	U	F	D	O	I	?	N	S
E	A	I	T	U	E	B	G	F	S	U	T
A	G	N	S	S	?						

The Stolen
Ark of God

Introduction

"Evening, and morning, and at noon, will I pray, and
cry aloud: and he shall hear my voice. . . . O how I love
thy law! It is my meditation all the day."

(Psalms 55:17; 119:97, KJV)

Do you have a best friend? How often do you see your
friend? If you began to pal around with other kids and
hardly ever spoke to your friend, would he still consider
himself your best friend? Would he come to help you if you
needed him? Probably not! Even if you reminded him of the
good times you used to have, he'd probably say, "Ask help
from those kids you hang out with now—not me."

If you love someone, you'll make time to be with that person. Thinking about your former good times won't keep a

friendship going. This can apply to our love for God, too. The Israelites learned this in the story of the stolen ark of God.

The Facts, Please!

1. At the foot of Mt. Sinai, the Israelites built the tabernacle by the directions God gave them. A fence of curtains surrounded the tent. This was the outer court, where the people worshiped God and the priests offered sacrifices on an altar for the sins of all the people. Inside the tabernacle a thick curtain divided two rooms. The outer room, the Holy Place, was where the priests went to perform certain duties in the worship of God. The inner room was the Holy of Holies, or the Most Holy Place. Only the high priest could enter there. Inside it was the ark of God.

2. The ark was a box, about 45 inches long, 27 inches wide, and 27 inches deep. It was made of wood and covered with gold. There were rings on the side, with long poles inserted in them, for carrying the ark. The ark was never to be removed from the Most Holy Place, unless God said to do it.

   Inside the ark were the stone tablets on which the Ten Commandments were written. The cover of the ark was pure gold. On it were two golden cherubim, facing each other, with their outstretched wings touching in the center. Underneath the wings was the mercy seat—the place where God met with his people. He showed his presence by a brilliant light above the mercy seat.

The high priest entered the Most Holy Place only once a year. Then he sprinkled the blood of a bull on the mercy seat. When he returned again, a shout of joy went up from the people, because that meant God had forgiven their sins of the past year.

Bible Story: The Ark of God in Enemy Territory
(1 Samuel 4:1-21)

The Israelites were in trouble again—bad trouble! In a battle with a great enemy, the Philistines, four thousand of their soldiers had been killed. It was a terrible defeat.

The Israelite army returned to their camp, and the leaders got together in a council of war. "Why did the Lord let the Philistines defeat us?" they asked. "We must have God's presence with us in the next battle."

"Let's take the ark of God out of the tabernacle," someone suggested. "If we take it along when we fight again, it will save us from our enemies."

The leaders agreed. Some men went to the tabernacle at Shiloh, marched right into the Most Holy Place, and walked out with the ark of God! The two sons of the priest, who were very wicked, went along to take care of it. "Here comes the ark into the camp!" someone yelled. All the soldiers lifted their voices in such a shout of joy that the earth shook with the sound.

The Philistines heard the noise. "What is that great noise in the camp of the Hebrews?" they asked.

Someone told them, "They have brought in the ark of God."

The Philistines were very frightened. "God has come into their camp!" they exclaimed. "Woe to us! Who can save us from the mighty gods of Israel? We must fight as we never fought before! If we don't we will be their slaves, just as they have been our slaves."

There was a fierce battle. The Philistines fought hard. They killed 30,000 Israelite footsoldiers and the two sons of the priest. Worst of all, they stole the ark and took it home with them. The holy ark of God was in enemy territory! In our next story we'll learn what happened to it there.

This Is for You

God's people lost their first battle with their enemies because they had drifted far away from God. They had sinned greatly and had not repented. They thought God would be with them and give them victory because their nation used to worship him. In the next battle, they took along the ark of God like a magic charm to help them win. No wonder they were defeated!

The Israelites were backsliders. They had stopped obeying and worshiping God. Still, they expected him to be with them when they needed him. A Christian can backslide, too. It doesn't happen all at once. It begins with failing to stay close to God by reading the Bible and praying every day. Soon God is not as important as he once was. It becomes easier to sin. Then, when things go wrong, the backslider asks, "Where is God? Why did he let these bad things happen to me?"

Where is God? Right where he always was. God hasn't gone away—the backslider has left him. If this has happened to us, we can repent and get right with God. We can begin to have daily Bible reading and prayer and to be faithful in church. Let's think about God and let him run our life. Then we'll feel him there when we need his help.

Unscramble Words:
A Palestine News Report

If there had been newspapers in the Holy Land, what might the headlines and the news story have been like after the terrible battle with the Philistines when the ark was stolen? Unscramble the letters, and place the correct words above the scrambled ones to tell what could have been said.

NEWS FLASH! THE __ __ __ OF __ __ __ IS __ __ __ __ __ __!
               K A R   D O G   N E L T O S

A terrific __ __ __ __ __ __ happened today near Ebenezer
       l e t b a t

between the __ __ __ __ __ __ __ __ __ army and the
        r a t e l e s i l

__ __ __ __ __ __ __ __ __ __ __. To make sure that God
t i P h i l i n e s s

would be with them, the Israelites took along the __ __ __
                          k a r

of __ __ __. A great __ __ __ __ __ went up from their
   d o G   t o u s h

__ __ __ __ __ when it arrived. But there was no __ __ __ __
m a p c   l e p h

from God. The __ __ __ __ __ __ __ __ __ __ __ fought very
          t i s P i i l n e s h

hard, and they __ __ __ __ __ __ __ __ __ __ __ __
          l e k l i d   r y i h t t

thousand Israelite __ __ __ __ soldiers. Then, worst of all,
       t o o f

215

they __ __ __ __ __ the __ __ __ of __ __ __. All hope is
     l o s e t   k a r   d o G
gone for its __ __ __ __ __ __ from enemy territory.
             t n e r r u

A Tipsy Idol,
Lowing Cows,
and Golden Rats

Introduction

"You shall not make yourselves any idols: no images of animals, birds, or fish. You must never bow or worship it in any way."

(Exodus 20:4-5, TLB)

THE book of Isaiah tells about a man who plants a tree, waters it, cares for it, and then cuts it down. He builds a fire with part of the wood to warm himself. With some more wood, he builds a fire to roast his meat. There is nothing strange about that. But what he does next is very odd. He takes the rest of his wood and carves out an idol and falls down and worships it, praying, "Deliver me; for you are my god."

Would you ever do something as foolish as that? Before

you answer, think about this story of a tipsy idol, lowing cows, and golden rats.

The Facts, Please!

1. The tipsy idol—This idol was Dagon, the main god of the Philistines. Its body or trunk was the likeness of a fish, and its top half was of a man, with arms and hands. Dagon was considered to be the father of another famous heathen god, Baal. The Philistines had two main temples in honor of Dagon—one at Ashdod, and one at Gaza, with smaller temples elsewhere.

2. Lowing cows—In Bible times the terms used in regard to cattle were the same as now: a male was a bull, a female was a cow, and their offspring was a calf. Before a female had any calves, she was known as a heifer, and the young male was a bullock. A milk cow was not accustomed to being yoked up to a cart. If her baby calf was penned up, she would do everything she could to go to where it was. It would be a very unnatural thing for her to walk away from her baby and her own pasture and pull a cart into a strange land.

3. Rats—Rats are rodents (gnawing animals). There are over five hundred kinds of rats all over the world. Rats are very destructive. They eat crops and pass along diseases to people. The black rat was responsible for spreading the Black Plague throughout Europe in the Middle Ages.

Bible Story: The Idol That Couldn't Stand Still
(1 Samuel 5:1–6:18)

"Ha, ha! The God of the Hebrews isn't so great," sneered the Philistines after their great battle with the Israelites. "We have captured the ark of God, and he couldn't stop us! We will place it in the temple of Dagon." They took the ark to the temple in Ashdod and set it before their idol.

The next morning they couldn't believe what they saw. Dagon had fallen with his face to the ground before the ark! They set him up again; but the next morning, Dagon was on the ground again before the ark. This time, his head and hands had been broken off and were lying in the doorway.

A terrible plague of rats destroyed the grain in their fields, and the people of Ashdod began to have awful boils on their bodies. They said, "The ark of God must not stay here any longer. His hand is heavy upon us and upon our god, Dagon."

The ark was sent to the city of Gath and then to Ekron. The people there, too, got the plague of boils. For seven months the ark remained in the land of the Philistines, and disease and death were everywhere.

At last the heathen priests and magicians advised, "You must make a new cart to carry the ark back to Israel. Hitch it up to two milk cows who have just had calves, and pen up their calves. Put gifts on the cart as a sin offering to the God of Israel. If the cows go on their own back to Israel, we will know that God caused them. If not, we'll know they just happened by chance."

The ark was placed on the new cart, along with gifts of five golden rats and five golden boils. Two cows were hitched to the cart. Away they went, lowing after their young calves, but still walking away from them. The Philistines followed them, watching to see where they would go.

The cows went straight to Beth Shemesh, a city of Israel. The people there saw the ark and shouted for joy. Then the Philistines knew that Israel's God, not Dagon, was the true God.

This Is for You

God allowed the ark to be captured to teach a lesson to the Israelites. Then he taught the Philistines that their idol wasn't all-powerful—the God of Israel was. The sad thing is that, even though they saw and recognized God's power, they did not turn from their idol worship and believe in him.

Isn't it strange that people could make something with their own hands and then fall down and worship it? You wouldn't do that, would you? But wait a minute! Idol worship isn't done just by heathen people. Even Christians can have idols. An idol is something that we ourselves make into a god. It is whatever we let come between us and God.

Are such things as money, clothing, good times, sports, or popularity more important to us than pleasing and serving God? Do they keep us from attending church? We must be careful! We don't want to be idol worshipers. If God is not Lord of all, he isn't Lord at all.

Finish the Poem:
An Idol or God?

Fill the blanks in the poem by printing the letters in the alphabet that come after the ones given in parentheses. For example, Ahakd would be Bible. (A follows Z.)

I would not worship _____ (hcnkr)

Of metal, wood, or _____; (rsnmd)

But do I worship other _____ (sghmfr)

Instead of God _____? (zknmd)

Whatever comes between _____, (tr)

My wondrous God and _____ (ld)

A place, a person, or a _____ (sghmf)

That can my idol _____. (ad)

Dear Jesus, I will choose _____ (xnt)

To be my Lord and _____. (Jhmf)

I want to put you first of _____ (zkk)

In each and every _____. (sghmf)

If this is your prayer to Jesus, sign your name here:

_____

The Raging Storm on the Sea of Galilee

Introduction

"The Lord himself goes before you and will be with you; he will never leave you nor forsake you. Do not be afraid; do not be discouraged."

(Deuteronomy 31:8)

In the British Museum is an old mariners' chart drawn up in 1525. It shows what people in that day thought the east coast of North America and its waters were like. Over large areas of land and sea still unexplored the chartmaker had written these words: "Here be fiery scorpions," "Here be dragons," "Here be giants." Later a scientist, Sir John Franklin, wrote across the map, "Here is God."

Of course, there were no scorpions, dragons, or giants. But even if there had been, God *was* there and could handle them. Believers don't need to fear either real or imagined dangers because God is present. The disciples learned about that one night in a raging storm on the Sea of Galilee.

The Facts, Please!

1. The Sea of Galilee is a lake whose waters are blue and sweet. They come from the Jordan River, which enters the lake by a steep descent. For over 25 miles the river falls at the rate of 60 feet for each mile to arrive at the lake.

2. The Bible gives four names for this lake: the Sea of Chinnereth, the Lake of Gennesaret, the Sea of Tiberias, and the Sea of Galilee. Jesus did many miracles on or around the Sea of Galilee.

3. This lake, about 13 miles long and 7 miles wide at its widest point, is shaped something like a harp. (The Hebrew word *chinnereth* means "harp-shaped".) Except on the southern side, the lake is surrounded by steep cliffs and mountains that rise sharply from its shores, some as high as 2,700 feet.

4. Sudden storms come in over the mountains and stir the water up into violent 20-foot waves. A boat can leave the shore in a calm sea and be caught in a vicious storm before reaching the other side.

5. Several of Jesus' disciples were fishermen who lived near the Sea of Galilee and earned their living by fishing in its waters. They were used to the frequent storms, but a storm came one evening that was not

like any they had ever seen. It frightened even those seasoned sailors.

Bible Story: Asleep in the Middle of a Storm
(Mark 4:35-41)

"Let's cross over to the other side of the lake," Jesus said to his disciples one evening. For several days, he had been teaching people and healing the sick as he traveled through Galilee. Now he was very tired.

Leaving the crowds behind, the disciples and Jesus stepped on board the fishing boat. While some of the disciples rowed, Jesus went to the back part of the boat, laid his head on the pillow there, and went to sleep.

Suddenly, without warning, a storm swooped down from the mountains. Fierce, howling winds battered the little boat about like a toy and whipped the waters of the lake into huge waves. They beat the boat until it was almost full of water and about to sink. The disciples were terrified. It was the worst storm they had ever seen! Where was Jesus? Why didn't he do something? They stumbled through the darkness against the force of the wind to find him.

There he was—still asleep on his pillow! How could he sleep in such a storm? They shouted above the noise of the winds and waves, "Master, Master, don't you care that we are dying?"

Jesus awoke and stood up. He looked out at the furious winds and rebuked them. He spoke to the angry waves, saying, "Peace, be still!" At once, there was only a gentle breeze and calm sea. "Why were you so fearful?" Jesus asked his disciples. "Where is your faith?"

The disciples were amazed. "Who is this man that even the winds and seas obey him?" they asked one another.

This Is for You

The disciples should have realized they didn't need to fear. The Creator and Master of the winds and seas was on their boat. The human body of Jesus was very tired, and he went to sleep, trusting his heavenly Father's care and protection. But he was more than human. As God, he arose and calmed the storm.

Jesus asked his disciples where their faith was. When they started the trip, he had said, "Let us go to the other side of the lake." Did they think he would take them to the middle of the lake to drown? He said they were going to the other side; so, even though there was a fierce storm, he took them there.

Our lives are like that little fishing boat. We won't always travel through calm and peaceful waters. Sometimes we will have rough, scary times. When real or imagined dangers come, we may be tempted to panic and be frightened. Don't forget who it is that is with us if we're God's children. Our heavenly Father is there! We can rest in him and smile at the storm.

No situation that we will ever face is too big for Jesus to handle. He will help us every time if we will ask him.

Coded Message:
God Calms the Storms of Life

The disciples should have remembered Psalm 107:23-31 when they were in the great storm. Those words also apply to the storms of life that may come our way. Read them for yourself and see what God will do. Then fill the blanks in the sentences below by adding or subtracting letters as directed. For example, A+3 is D.

A B C D E F G H I J K L M N O P Q R S T U V W X Y Z

Those who ___ ___ ___ ___ on the ___ ___ ___ in
        p+3 b-1 k-2 o-3   t-1 c+2 f-5

___ ___ ___ ___ ___ see the works of the Lord and his
r+1 j-2 g+2 o+1 t-1

___ ___ ___ ___ ___ ___ ___ in the deep. The stormy
y-2 n+1 l+2 g-3 f-1 n+4 q+2

___ ___ ___ ___ ___ lift the ___ ___ ___ ___ ___ high.
z-3 h+1 m+1 b+2 t-1   z-3 e-4 u+1 g-2 r+1

Their ships rise up to the ___ ___ ___ ___ ___ ___ ___ and
        j-2 d+1 b-1 s+3 g-2 m+1 q+2

sink down into the ___ ___ ___ ___ ___ ___. The sailors
      c+1 h-3 o+1 w-3 i-1 r+1

are at their ___ ___ ___ ___' end. They ___ ___ ___ to the
      v+1 n-5 s+1 q+2   d-1 q+1 w+2

Lord, and he ___ ___ ___ ___ ___ the storm. Then they are
      a+2 b-1 j+2 p-3 r+1

___ ___ ___ ___, and the Lord brings them safely to their
h-1 o-3 b-1 i-5

___ ___ ___ ___ ___ ___. ___ ___ ___ ___ ___ ___ the
f+2 c-2 q+1 a+1 l+3 q+1 N+2 o+3 c-2 j-1 r+1 h-3
Lord for his wonderful ___ ___ ___ ___ ___ to ___ ___ ___!
      x-1 l+3 p+2 j+1 t-1 z-1 l+3 v-1

39

Life for a Look at a Snake

Introduction

"Just as Moses lifted up the snake in the desert, so the Son of Man must be lifted up, that everyone who believes in him may have eternal life."

(John 3:14-15)

Suppose a man accidentally swallowed some deadly poison. He would get very sick and would soon die if he didn't have an antidote for the poison. A bottle of antidote was within his reach, but he refused to take it. After much agony, the man died. Whose fault was it?

Hundreds, maybe thousands, of people were poisoned one time. They were bitten by poisonous snakes. Even though they were far from a hospital or doctors, a remedy was provided for them. Some people took it, but probably some did not.

The Facts, Please!

1. Snakes are legless reptiles. Scientists believe there are over three thousand kinds of snakes in the world at this time. The greatest number and the largest ones are found in warmer climates, but a few kinds can also be found in cold, mountainous regions. Most snakes live on land. Some, like the water moccasin, live on land and in water. Sea snakes live in water. There are even snakes who make their home in trees.

2. Snakes range in length from 5 inches or less to 30 feet. All snakes are covered with scales that keep their bodies from losing too much moisture. Their eyes are covered with a transparent cap that keeps them open all the time. They do not have movable eyelids. A snake keeps flicking out its long, forked tongue while moving along the ground. It is collecting sensations of touch and smell.

   A snake's spine may contain as many as three hundred tiny vertebrae, each with a pair of ribs. The jaws of a snake are very loosely attached to each other and to the skull. For this reason it can swallow whole an animal two or three times as thick as its head. It doesn't chew its food, but its stomach juices digest all of the animal except feathers and hairs.

3. Only about 8 out of 100 snakes are harmful to man.

Some are helpful because they kill pests like rats and mice.

4. The Sinai Desert has several kinds of snakes. Some of these hide in the sand and attack without warning. We don't know what kind of snake the "fiery serpent" in our story was. They may have been called "fiery" because of their bright color, the burning sensations produced by the deadly poison of their bite, or the hot fever that burned in its victims.

Bible Story: Fiery Snakes and a Snake of Healing
(Numbers 21:4-9)

"Why have you brought us out here in the wilderness to die?" the Israelites grumbled to Moses. "We don't have any bread, and we hate this manna God gave us." It had been about 40 years since the children of Israel had left Egypt to go to the "land flowing with milk and honey." They could have gone into the Promised Land many years before, but they were afraid of the giants there and didn't trust God to protect them. All that time God had taken care of his people. He had provided water when there was none. He had sent manna for bread and quail for meat. And this was the thanks he got!

Because of their complaining, God sent fiery snakes that suddenly appeared in their camp. They were everywhere—in the tents and outside on the ground. No one could escape them. Many people died. The Israelites stopped grumbling and came to Moses. "We have sinned against the Lord

231

and you," they said. "Please ask God to take away these snakes."

Moses prayed to God. "Make a brass snake that looks like the fiery serpents and set it on a pole where everyone can see it," God told Moses. "Every person who has been bitten by the snakes may look at the brass snake and be healed."

Moses followed God's instructions and set up the pole with the brass snake on it. And, sure enough, if a person who had been bitten believed God and looked at the snake, he was healed right away. If a poisoned person did not believe God and look, he died. There was life for a look at a snake!

This Is for You

One night Jesus told Nicodemus about being born again. "Just as Moses lifted up the snake in the desert, so the Son of Man must be lifted up," he said. "Everyone who believes in him may have eternal life." When was Jesus lifted up? When he died on the cross.

Satan is called a serpent in the Bible. The snake's bite is like sin, which Satan helped bring into the world. We have all been poisoned by sin because we were born sinners and each of us has sinned. The brass snake looked like the fiery snakes, but it had no poison in it. Jesus never sinned, but he became sin for us when he took our sin on himself as he died on the cross. Now anyone who believes in him will be saved from sin.

Jesus died for us. He will take away our sin and its punishment if we will believe in him as our Savior. Just one look of belief at Jesus—that's all it takes. Look and live!

Coded Verse:
Sin's Wages or God's Gift

Write down, in the order in which they appear in the chart, the letters for each symbol. You will have written Romans 6:23 from the King James Version. Have you received God's gift?

♥	🎁	♡	†	♥	♡	🎁	†	♡	♥	🎁
F	d	i	J	o	s	e	e	e	r	a
†	♥	♡	🎁	†	♡	♥	🎁	♡	🎁	♥
s	t	t	t	u	e	h	h	r	b	e
†	🎁	♥	♡	†	♥	🎁	♡	♥	♡	🎁
s	u	w	n	C	a	t	a	g	l	t
♥	†	🎁	♡	†	🎁	♡	♥	†	♡	†
e	h	h	l	r	e	i	s	i	f	s
🎁	♥	♡	🎁	†	♥	♡	🎁	♡	♥	♡
g	o	e	i	t	f	t	f	h	s	r
†	🎁	♡	♥	†	🎁	♡	♥	†	†	🎁
o	t	o	i	u	o	u	n	r	L	f
†	♥	♡	🎁	†	♥	♡	🎁	†	🎁	
o	i	g	G	r	s	h	o	d	d	

♥ _____

🎁 _____

♡ _____

† _____

The Bread That Satisfied

Introduction

"Then Jesus declared, 'I am the bread of life. He who comes to me will never go hungry, and he who believes in me will never be thirsty.'"

(John 6:35)

A preacher and some other guests were invited to a farm home for Sunday dinner. There was not enough room at the table for everybody at once, so the farmer's little boy had to wait until the others had eaten. "But, Mama," he said, "what if they don't leave me any fried chicken?"

"Oh, they'll leave a piece on the plate for manners' sake," replied his mother.

The little boy watched as piece after piece of fried chicken was taken. Finally, the preacher reached out and took the only remaining drumstick. "Well, there goes the last piece—manners and all," the boy said, with a sigh.

Have you ever been at a meal where there wasn't enough food to satisfy everyone's hunger? This happened one time at Elisha's school of prophets when there wasn't enough bread.

The Facts, Please!

1. Bread was a very important part of a Jewish meal in Bible times. For most people, the main meal consisted of bread, cheese, fruit, and vegetables. Meat was not eaten often. Bread was so important that the term "eating bread" meant "having a meal."

2. The best bread was made from wheat. A cheaper, coarser bread was made from barley.

3. After the grain had been ground into flour on a hand mill, the flour was mixed with water and kneaded on a small kneading trough. Unleavened bread was then baked into thin, round cakes that were quite hard. To make leavened bread, a piece of dough from the previous batch was added to the new dough. The leavened lump was left by the fire, sometimes all night, to let the dough rise. The dough was divided into round cakes that looked something like round stones, about nine inches across and as thick as a finger. Then it was baked on flat stones or in a simple earthenware oven, heated over a fire.

4. God told the Israelites to take some of the first grain

that they harvested and give it to the Lord. This was called the firstfruits. It could be in the form of the grain itself or baked into bread.

Bible Story: How 100 Hungry Men Were Fed
(2 Kings 4:42-44)

At Elisha's school of the prophets, 100 hungry men sat down at the table. But there was no food. There was a famine in the land, and food was hard to come by.

About that time, a man came to see Elisha. "I have just begun harvesting my barley," he said. "You are a man of God, so I am bringing my firstfruits to you to feed the young prophets." The man gave Elisha 20 loaves of barley bread and some grain.

Elisha thanked the man and then called his servant, Gehazi. "Give this to the men, so they may eat," Elisha said.

Gehazi's eyes opened wide in surprise. "What? You want me to feed 100 hungry men with this little bit of food?"

"Give this to the men," Elisha repeated. "The Lord says there will be plenty for all to eat, and there will be some left." Gehazi set the few small loaves and the kernels of grain on the table, and the men began to eat. They ate and ate until everyone was satisfied. And there was food left over, just as God had said.

This Is for You

How could 20 small loaves feed 100 hungry men? Perhaps God enlarged the loaves; we don't know. But somehow he made it to be enough. Every man went away completely satisfied.

Many people in the world today are hungry for food; some are even starving. Those of us who have plenty of food should do what we can to help them. But there is another hunger that's even worse than that. It is a sinner's soul hunger. Sinners don't have the joy of knowing that their sins are forgiven and that they will have a home in heaven someday. They don't have a heavenly Father to take care of them and supply their needs. They don't have the peace that Jesus gives. Jesus said, "I am the Bread of Life, Whoever comes to me will never hunger. Those who believe in me will never thirst." He completely satisfies soul hunger.

A man brought the bread to Elisha, and Gehazi gave it to the men. God made it satisfy them. We can tell sinners about Jesus. If they will take him as Savior, he will supply all their spiritual needs. Will we be good witnesses for Jesus? Will we tell as many as we can about the Bread that satisfies?

Word Search:
100 Hungry Men Satisfied

Find and circle the listed words from the story. You can go down or across.

barley	hundred	men
bread	hungry	satisfied
Elisha	kernels	table
God	loaves	

```
L G O D T A B L E
O E L I S H A T W
A L H U N D R E D
V K E R N E L S O
E M E N B R E A D
S H U N G R Y I N
S A T I S F I E D
```

Sweeter than Honey

Introduction

"No, I haven't turned away from what you taught me; your words are sweeter than honey."

(Psalm 119:102-103, TLB)

SOME people know the Bible about as well as a little girl named Jill did. A preacher came to call at her home. While waiting for her mother to come out, he asked Jill, "Do you go to Sunday school?" When she said she did, the preacher picked up a Bible that was on the table. "Then can you tell me something that's in this book?" he asked.

"Sure, I can," replied Jill. "I know everything that's in it. There's Mom's recipe for fried chicken, a picture of Grandma, a lock of my hair when I was a baby, and Dad's birthday card from Aunt Sarah."

Do you know what's in your Bible—what's really in it? If you'll read and study it regularly, you'll find something in it that is sweeter than honey.

THE FACTS, PLEASE!

1. The Israelites left Egypt to go into Canaan—a land that God said flowed with milk and honey. There were rich pasturelands for cows and many flowers to give food to honeybees. Ancient people had no sugar, so honey was a great treat to the Jews. It was their major sweetening substance.

2. Bees are the only insects that produce food for man. Each honeybee has six legs, five eyes, two slender antennae (which serve as a nose, with two thousand to three thousand tiny sense plates), four very thin wings, a stinger, and a mouth. The tongue of the worker bee is like a tube, through which it can sip nectar.

3. The worker bees locate flowers and obtain nectar (a sugary liquid), which is stored in their honey bag. On the way to the hive, the nectar in the bag changes to a sweet, thick liquid. When stored in the wax honeycomb, it dries into honey.

4. A red clover blossom contains less than one-eighth of a grain of sugar. Seven thousand grains are required to make a pound of honey. A bee must sip from 3,360,000 flowerets in 56,000 clover heads to get one pound.

5. In New Testament times, a schoolboy received a slate with Bible passages written on it. Honey was smeared on his slate, and he had to trace the letters through the honey with his pen. Since he would naturally lick off the honey, it was hoped he would realize that the Scriptures must be absorbed and enjoyed.

Bible Story: Why the Jews Had a Celebration
(Nehemiah 8:1-18)

"Let's call the people together and read the Book of God to them. It has been a long, long time since they have heard it," Nehemiah said to Ezra, the priest. It had been 70 years since the Jews had been carried away as captives to Babylon. Now some of them had returned to their own land.

Word was sent to all the Jews in Jerusalem and nearby cities and villages to come to the temple. A great company of men, women, and older children gathered in a plaza in front of the Water Gate, near the southeast corner of the temple. "Read the law of God that he gave to Moses," they said to Ezra. He climbed on a wooden stand, high above the heads of the people, with the scroll of Moses' law in his hand.

When Ezra opened the scroll, everyone stood up. "Praise the Lord, the great God!" Ezra called out. "Amen! Amen!" shouted all the people. They bowed their heads to the ground and worshiped. As Ezra read each sentence, priests and Levites explained the meaning of the words, some of them on the stand and some in the crowd. Ezra read from early morning until noon. Many of the people had never heard the law of God read before. They learned that they had committed many sins, and they began to weep loudly. "Don't cry," Nehemiah and Ezra told them. "This is a holy day. It is a time to be very happy because you have heard and understood God's Book. Go home and eat and drink and send food to those who don't have any."

So everyone had a joyful celebration. For the next seven days they lived in booths of branches and leaves and listened to the reading of the Scriptures daily. They confessed their sins and began to obey God. Truly, his Word had been sweeter than honey to them!

This Is for You

Here are three ways we could read the Bible: (1) Like taking bitter medicine—not enjoyable but we know we need it. (2) Like eating shredded wheat biscuits—dry but nourishing. (3) Like sipping honey—enjoyable, nourishing, and sweet. We'll only get the honey by taking time to read the Bible and letting God talk to us through it.

God's laws don't rob us of our fun and good times. They are for our good. They warn us of the dangers of sinning. They light our path and show us the right way to go. They tell us how to have a happy, productive life.

The Bible helps us solve many problems in our daily lives. Are we sad? It tells us how to have joy. Are we upset and troubled? It shows us the way to find peace, even when things go wrong. Are we tempted to sin? It guides us in handling temptation. Do we feel no one cares what happens to us? We can find comfort by reading it. The more we read and absorb the words of God's Book, the sweeter they will become—sweeter than honey, dripping from a honeycomb.

Crossword Puzzle:
What the Jews Did When They Heard God's Book

Fill in the blanks as you solve the crossword puzzle.

The Jews _____ together. They _____ to the ground
      (6 down)   (2 down)
and _____ God. They _____ to the reading of God's
   (7 across)   (8 across)
Book. They _____ over their sins. They _____ and
      (3 down)   (5 down)
_____ in a joyful celebration. They _____ food to the
 (9 across)   (4 across)
poor. They _____ that they heard and understood God's
      (1 down)
laws.

42

The Stolen Spear and Jug of Water

Introduction

"Love your enemies, bless them that curse you, do good to them that hate you, and pray for them which despitefully use you, and persecute you."

(Matthew 5:44, KJV)

HAVE you ever had an enemy—someone who keeps on doing mean, nasty things to you, even if you haven't done anything to cause him or her to act like that? How do you treat that person?

"I don't understand your attitude about your enemies," someone said to President Lincoln one day. "Why do you try to make friends of them? You should try to destroy them."

"I am destroying my enemies," Mr. Lincoln replied, "when I make them my friends."

Do you know of a better way to get rid of your enemies? Even if you can't make a friend out of an enemy, you can try. That is what David did when he stole King Saul's spear and jug of water.

The Facts, Please!

1. Spear—In Bible times, spears were important fighting weapons. They were used by all ancient nations. A spear is a weapon with a long, slender shaft (pole or handle), tipped with a metal or stone point. It is similar to a javelin but larger and heavier. A warrior would either throw one at an enemy or thrust it into him.

2. Once, when David was playing his harp for King Saul, the king in a jealous rage threw a spear at him. Saul meant to pin David to the wall, but David jumped aside. This may have been the very same spear that David stole from Saul later on.

3. Jug of water—King Saul had a jug of water by his head as he lay sleeping on the ground. According to an ancient custom, a high official would provide a king with a very expensive urn that contained water for him to use when he was on a journey or in warfare. To lose this special water jug to an enemy would be an embarrassment and a disgrace for a king.

Bible Story: David Spares His Sleeping Enemy's Life
(1 Samuel 26:1-25)

King Saul was out to get David. Saul knew that someday soon David would be the king, so he was determined to kill David and be rid of him once and for all. He had tried several times already to kill David, but each time David escaped. Saul, with his army, searched everywhere for David and his four hundred followers. The soldiers looked in the caves and hills of the rough, mountainous country near the Dead Sea where David hid out, but David always eluded them.

One day some men came to Saul and said, "David and his men are hiding on the hill of Hakilah." Saul took his army of three thousand men and camped out near the hill. When David heard they were there, he sent out spies to see what Saul was doing.

At night Saul and his men slept out on the ground. The king and his general, Abner, slept inside a circle of baggage wagons. His troops slept in a ring all around them. Surely, Saul must have thought, he was safe from any harm there!

After dark, David asked one of his soldiers, Abishai, to go with him to Saul's camp. Abishai agreed, and the two of them quietly sneaked into the camp of their enemies. No soldier stirred, for God had sent a deep sleep on all of them.

David and Abishai came right up to where Saul was sleeping. His spear was stuck in the ground near his head. "God has given your enemy into your hands this time," whispered Abishai to David. "Let me put that spear through him, right to the ground. I won't need to do it twice!"

"No," whispered David. "He is God's anointed king. I won't kill him. God will do it someday, or he'll die in battle. Take his spear and his jug of water, and we'll leave." The two men slipped back out of camp and sped away with the spear and the jug. Still, no one in Saul's camp moved.

David and Abishai climbed up on the top of a hill, overlooking the camp. Then David called out loudly, "Abner! Why haven't you taken care of your king? Didn't you know that someone came right up to him to kill him? Look for his spear and jug of water. Are they there?"

Saul and Abner, startled out of sleep, looked around. Sure enough, his spear and jug of water were gone! They knew that David had stolen them. He could have killed Saul, but he didn't. But before long, God caused the wicked king to die in battle, just as David had said.

This Is for You

David let God take care of his enemy. Does that mean it's always wrong to defend ourselves from those who want to harm us? Not at all. Sometimes it's necessary to protect ourselves. David didn't need to do that then because his enemy was asleep. Did David make a friend of his enemy? No, but he tried.

When someone does us wrong, it's natural to want to get even. But it's not Christlike. What did Jesus do when the wicked men nailed him to a cross? He said, "Father, forgive them, for they don't know what they're doing." He loved those men, and he was dying for their sins. He would have saved any of them, if they had asked him to do it.

Only God can give us the power to do good to those who harm us, to love them, and to forgive them. We can ask him to help us try our best to make a friend out of our enemies.

Letter Maze:
David's Secret Night Mission

In wartime, many secret missions are carried out at night. Under the cover of darkness, David and Abishai sneaked into Saul's camp and out again to a nearby hill. With a pencil, trace their path by following the letters of the words "Saul's spear and jug of water" twice in the proper order.

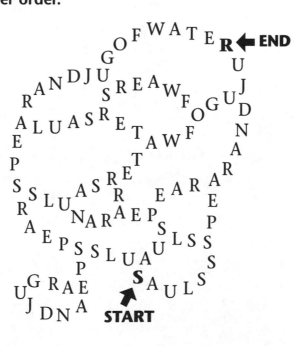

251

Two Spies
in a Well

Introduction

"A true friend is always loyal, and a brother is born to
help in time of need. . . . The greatest love is shown
when a person lays down his life for his friends."

(Proverbs 17:17; John 15:13, TLB)

WOULD you say that a really good friend is one who sticks
by you like a shadow? That's being very close! But think
again. When does a shadow go with you? When you're in
sunlight or moonlight. Where is the shadow when you're
not in the light? A real friend is one who sticks by you when
things look dark and dreary and aren't going well. He'll be
there when you need help and encouragement, no matter
what the cost to himself.

One time King David desperately needed friends like that.

And he did have some who stuck by him. As two of them risked their lives to help him, they had to hide in a well to escape his enemies.

The Facts, Please!

1. Usually a well is a pit or hole dug into the earth to provide water. Different kinds of wells are mentioned in the Bible, including some that are just natural sources of water. There are cisterns, pits, springs, and fountains.

2. In the hot, dry climate of Palestine and nearby countries, wells were very important. People who kept large herds of cattle and flocks of sheep especially needed them. In the summer drought when most other sources of water were dried up, animals had to be watered at wells. In villages, a well was the center of activity. People went there, usually in the morning or evening, to get their daily supply of water in leather buckets or in pottery pitchers. Usually the older, unmarried girls went for the water.

3. If a person was well-off, he might have his own well on his property. Alongside the well, a cistern was dug in which the water could be stored when drawn from the well. At the end of the summer, when the cistern was dry, it could make a good hiding place.

Bible Story: The Spies' Secret Hiding Place
(2 Samuel 15:13-37; 16:15-23; 17:1-29; 18:1-17)

Absalom, the third son of King David, was very handsome, with long, heavy hair that hung down over his shoulders.

David loved Absalom very much, but Absalom was not a faithful son. Behind David's back, he won the hearts of many of the people to himself and away from David. One day they crowned Absalom king in the city of Hebron.

When David heard about it, he gathered his family and servants together and left his palace in Jerusalem in a hurry. "Absalom will come soon with a big army to take over the city," David said. Six hundred brave men, who were still loyal to David, went with him.

The high priests, Zadok and Abiathar, went along. "I want you to go back to Jerusalem," David told them. "Absalom won't harm you, and you can be my spies. When you learn what Absalom is going to do, send your sons to tell me his plans."

Soon a secret agent of David's came to the priests and said, "Absalom is getting up a huge army. Tell David he must cross over the Jordan River and go into the wilderness. If he doesn't, he and all his army will die!"

Jonathan and Ahimaaz, the priests' sons, stayed outside the city walls, near a fountain, ready to carry messages to David. When the priests sent a servant girl to give the two men the important message, they hurried away. A boy saw them and ran to Absalom. "I saw some men that I think are spies," he said. Absalom sent some servants to follow them and arrest them.

Jonathan and Ahimaaz realized they were in danger. When they came to a house, they hid in a cistern. The woman of the house put a cloth over top of the well and covered it with grain to dry in the sun. As Jonathan and Ahimaaz crouched in the cistern, they heard Absalom's servants arrive and ask for them. Would the woman tell on them? No! She sent them on their way.

The spies reached David with the message. Quickly, he and all his people crossed the river that night. Soon there was a great battle in the woods. Absalom's army was beaten, and he was killed. David became king again because he had some loyal friends who didn't desert him when the going got tough.

This Is for You

King David had two kinds of friends—those who deserted him when they thought they would gain more by following Absalom, and those who were loyal to him, even to the point of risking their lives. The first ones were fair-weather friends. The others were true friends.

Are we fair-weather friends? Or do we stick by our friends and help them when they have troubles and problems? We must ask ourselves, "What kind of friends would my friends be if they were friends just like me?" Let's treat our friends the way we would want them to treat us.

Jesus set an example of true friendship; he gave his life for us. We may never have to die for a friend, but we can love our friends in the good and bad times and always be there when they need us. They'll be there to help us in the same way.

Match-up:
Friend or Foe?

In the list below there are names of people involved in this story about David and Absalom. Some are named in the Bible but not in the story as given here. (You can check the verses noted in the Bible story if you like.) Which ones were David's friends and which were his foes? By their description, print in the blanks either "friend" or "foe," depending on which you think they were.

1. Absalom: David's son who made himself king.
_____

2. Six hundred men: Brave men who went with David when he fled from Jerusalem. _____

3. Zadok and Abiathar: Priests who went with David, but returned to gather news and send it to him. _____

4. Jonathan and Ahimaaz: Sons of the priests and spies for David who risked their lives to bring him news.
_____

5. Many of David's former friends: They followed after Absalom. _____

6. Hushai: David's secret agent who stayed with Absalom to give him bad advice and send messages to David.
_____

7. A servant girl: She slipped out of the city to bring a message for the spies to take to David. _____

8. Ahithophel: A counselor of David who turned against him and gave advice to Absalom. _____

9. A woman: She hid the spies in her cistern and would not tell Absalom's servants where they were. _____

The Escape over a Wall in a Basket

Introduction

"I have fought a good fight, I have finished my course, I have kept the faith: Henceforth there is laid up for me a crown of righteousness."

(2 Timothy 4:7-8, KJV)

Do you remember the story about the race of the tortoise and the hare? The fast hare sprinted easily ahead of the slow, lumbering tortoise. But, thinking he had plenty of time, he took a nap. The tortoise just kept a-goin'. He passed by the snoozing hare and won the race.

Perhaps you've seen a footrace on TV where long after the other runners have reached the goal, a disabled person crept past the finish line—totally exhausted. He kept on keeping on, and he made it!

These are lessons in perseverance—in not giving up. Paul kept serving Christ, no matter what happened to him. Once he had to escape his enemies by going over a wall in a basket.

Thε Facts, Plεasε!

1. Walls—Many cities in ancient times were surrounded by walls for protection from enemies and even from dangerous wild animals. A city without a wall was considered defenseless. Walls were thick, high structures. They were usually made of earth or clay bricks that were mixed with reeds and hardened in the sun. Some walls were stone. Archaeologists have discovered remains of huge walls. Ninevah's wall was so wide that three chariots could ride on it side by side. The wall of Babylon was 87 feet wide—enough for six chariots riding side-by-side! Sometimes houses were built on top of a wall or into its sides, with windows of the houses looking out through the wall. The people who lived inside a wall felt safe and secure.

2. Baskets—These were containers of various sizes, shapes, and construction. Perhaps most often they were woven of fiber from leaves of palm or willow trees, from palm-tree twigs, or from rushes. Sometimes they were made of a mixture of clay and straw. Baskets were used to hold bread or carry fruits. Stronger, larger baskets carried grains or clay for making bricks. Some were even large enough to hold a man!

Bible Story: Paul over the Wall
(Acts 9:17-25; 2 Corinthians 11:26-33)

"Have you heard the news, Brother?" one Christian said to another. "Paul, the man who has put so many Christians in jail, is here in Damascus now. Perhaps we'll be his next victims!"

"Oh, we don't need to fear him," said the other Christian. "Brother Ananias says that Paul has believed in Jesus as his Savior, and he has been baptized. Why, he even preached in the synagogue that Jesus is the Son of God!"

It was true. On the way to Damascus, Paul had seen a light brighter than the noonday sun and had heard Jesus speaking to him. Right then he believed that Jesus is the Son of God and trusted him as his Savior. At once, he began to tell others about him. He had become the Christians' friend.

But the Jews who did not believe in Jesus were now Paul's enemies. "Isn't this the one who persecuted Jesus' followers in Jerusalem?" they asked. "Didn't he come here to arrest them all and take them to prison? What has happened to him?"

No matter what people said, Paul kept on preaching. He grew bolder in proving that Jesus was truly God's Son, and the Jews didn't know how to answer him. Paul left at that time and spent some time in Arabia. Then he came back to Damascus. When he again preached about Jesus, the Jews determined to kill him. They asked the governor to put guards at the city gates day and night to keep Paul from escaping.

One dark night the Christians sneaked Paul into a house on the city wall. They attached ropes to a huge basket, and

Paul got inside. Very quietly and carefully, strong men held the ropes and eased Paul through the window and down the side of the wall. When his basket hit the ground with a *thud*, he crawled out. Looking around to be sure he was safe, he tiptoed through the shadows until he was out of sight and sound of the guards. Then he hurried away. Where? To preach somewhere else.

This Is for You

Paul kept on serving God. He was the first missionary to the Gentiles and preached for many years. In spite of hardships and persecutions, he let nothing stop him from running the Christian race. Before he died he said, "I have finished my course, I have kept the faith, and I will win a prize."

Right now, if we're Christians, we have begun to run our life's race for Jesus' sake. What kind of runners will we be—like the hare or the tortoise? Will we finish our race, having done what God wants us to do, no matter how hard it is? We can begin now by being faithful in the little things. We can read our Bible, pray every day, go to church regularly, witness every chance we get, obey our parents and teachers, and do our best work at school. Like an athlete in training, doing these things will develop our spiritual muscles. They will prepare us for greater tasks ahead.

Don't get sidetracked. Keep a-goin' and win that crown!

Unscramble the Letters:
What Dangers Was Paul In?

Unscramble the letters below each line that describe Paul's dangers and suffering so he could be a witness for Jesus.

He was in danger in _____, with _____, from
(STAWER)   (BBERRSO)

his own _____ and from the Gentiles, in the _____ ,
(LEPPOE)   (TICIES)

in the _____, and in the _____. He was
(TRESDE)   (ASE)

_____ and in _____ from his labors and toils, he
(AWYER)   (NIPA)

watched through nights when he had no _____. He
(EPSEL)

was _____, _____, and didn't have enough
(GURNYH) (TRTYISH)

_____ to keep him warm.
(LSCOEHT)

Going Fishing

Introduction

"Be careful to do what the Lord your God has commanded you; do not turn aside to the right or to the left."
(Deuteronomy 5:32)

HAVE you ever heard the song that says, "I did it my way," or the one that says, "Everything's going my way"? Today there are teachings that say you are your own god. You are encouraged to do with your life whatever seems good to you.

We are not gods; we are human beings who can make mistakes. Only the true God in heaven knows everything. The only right way to go in life is the way he directs us to go. When we go his way—not ours—we'll have success. Some disciples learned about that one day when Jesus told them to go fishing.

The Facts, Please!

1. Fishing was a big business in Palestine when Jesus was on earth. Saltwater fish were caught in the Mediterranean and freshwater fish in the Sea of Galilee and smaller bodies of water. There was a large market for fish, and the industry grew so much around the Sea of Galilee that there were cities and villages all around its shoreline.

2. Fish were caught by several methods. Rod-and-line fishing was done with a pole, a line, and a hook of bone or iron. Spearfishing was often done at night. A lantern was held over the prow of the boat, which would attract fish to its light, and the fish were speared. Net fishing was done with either cast or seine nets. This method was used most often.

3. A cast net had a fine mesh and was circular, about 15 feet in diameter. The outer edges were weighted with lead sinkers. A long piece of fishing line was attached to the center, which a fisherman held with his left hand. When he saw a school of fish in shallow water, he threw the net over it and trapped the fish inside. Then he drew up the center of the net by the fishing line and dragged the fish to shore.

4. A seine net was about eight feet wide and hundreds of feet long and was suspended in the water like a fence, with corks at the top and weights at the bottom. Two boats would be used, each one having one end of the net. The fishermen would draw up the

bottom of the net to enclose the fish, putting them in the boats or bringing them to shore.

Bible Story: A Surprising Catch of Fish
(Luke 5:1-11)

Four fishermen went out in their boats on the Sea of Galilee one night hoping to net a good catch of fish. Andrew, Simon Peter, James, and John cast their nets again and again, but brought them up empty each time. All night long they worked. As the sun came up, they rowed back to land and began to clean their nets.

Soon Jesus came near, followed by a great throng of people who crowded near him to hear the Word of God. Seeing the two empty fishing boats, Jesus stepped into Simon Peter's boat. "Please push your boat out into the water a little way so that I may sit and speak to the people," Jesus said.

Jesus' voice rang out over the water to the crowds on the hillside near the shore. When he was through speaking, he said to Simon Peter, "Now row out to deeper water and let down your nets for a great catch of fish."

Simon Peter must have been surprised that Jesus wanted to go fishing with him. But he was sure there were no fish to be caught. "Master," he said, "we have fished all night long, and we have caught nothing. Just the same, because you say so, I will let down the net."

Simon Peter cast out the net and felt a tremendous tug. The net was loaded with fish! It began to break. "John! James! Come quickly!" he called. "Help us bring these fish to land." The two men brought their boat near Simon Peter's boat, and they filled both boats with fish until they almost sank.

Simon Peter was amazed. He knew that no one but the Creator of the fish could command them to go into his net like that. He fell at Jesus' feet and said, "O Lord, I am full of sin! You must leave me!"

"Don't be afraid," Jesus told him. "From now on, you will fish for men." Right then, Simon Peter left his boat and his nets to be a full-time follower of Jesus.

This Is for You

When Jesus told him to let down his nets and catch fish, Simon Peter could have said, "Well, I think I know more than you do about fishing. You've been a carpenter. What do you know about fishing?" He could have said that, but he didn't. He called Jesus "Master." He was saying that Jesus was the Captain of his boat and the one who should give the orders. When Simon Peter obeyed Jesus, he caught many fish. Instead of saying, "I'll do it my way," he did it Jesus' way. That's when he had success.

Are we afraid that Jesus will ask us to do something that will make us miserable? Remember two things: Jesus loves us, and he knows what is best for us. Going his way will bring us true happiness and the right kind of success. If you say, "I want to run my own life," think what happens when you put "I" in the middle of "run." It spells "ruin!"

Find the Right Words:
Peter's Wonderful Statement

Simon Peter and the other disciples failed to catch fish. But not after Peter made Jesus the Captain of his boat! In the word list below, cross out any words that appear more than two times. The remaining words fit in order (from left to right and top to bottom) on the blank lines and give Peter's statement, found in the King James Version of the Bible.

Master	you	fish	we	have
boat	toiled	you	all	fish
the	fish	night	and	you
have	boat	taken	nothing	boat
nevertheless	you	fish	at	thy
boat	word	I	fish	will
let	fish	down	the	net

" _____

_____

_____."

The Prison of No Escape

Introduction

"So let us come boldly to the very throne of God and stay there to receive his mercy and to find grace to help us in our times of need."

(Hebrews 4:16, TLB)

Can you solve this riddle? Suppose you were sealed in a prison room where there were no doors, windows, or any other kind of openings. You have no tools with which to dig, cut, or hammer a hole through the floors, walls, or ceiling. How could you get out? (Answer: You could break out with the measles!)

You will probably never be locked up in a prison. But you will have problems at times in your life, and you may think there is no way out. Peter had a problem like that one time—

when he was in a real prison. It seemed to be a prison of no escape.

The Facts, Please!

1. Ancient prisons were places of horror. They were gloomy, crude, rat-infested dungeons. They were dirty and had no proper ventilation. Some prisons were so cramped and small that the prisoner could not even stand up straight.
2. At first, the most common types of prisons were natural pits or caves. Cisterns, if there was no water in them, were sometimes used. Later, there were man-made prison houses.
3. In New Testament times, when the Romans ruled Palestine, prisons were often part of the government headquarters or of a king's palace.
4. Roman guards were responsible to see that their prisoners didn't escape. If they did, the guards could lose their lives.
5. The King Herod of this story (the grandson of the Herod who tried to kill Baby Jesus) hated Christians and tried to get rid of them.

Bible Story: Peter Escapes from the "Prison of No Escape"
(Acts 12:1-19)

King Herod was very pleased with himself. His soldiers had just cut off the head of one of Jesus' disciples, James. "Ha, ha!" he laughed gleefully. "The Jews are very happy about this! It has made them like me more than ever because they hate the Christians, too. I know what I'll do next. I'll put Peter in prison. Then, after the Jewish holiday is over, I'll bring him out and kill him, too."

Soon Peter was sitting in a dark prison cell, chained at the wrists to two Roman guards. All doors were securely locked. Outside, there were two more guards. Beyond that, there was a huge iron gate that was barred securely. Surely, it was a prison of no escape!

Several days went by. Then Herod said, "Tomorrow I'll bring Peter out of prison and kill him." There was no hope for Peter, no hope at all—except the Christians were all praying for Peter. Hour by hour they met together and asked God to deliver him. That last night they met at John Mark's house and prayed right on into the night.

What was Peter doing? Was his stomach tied up in knots because this was his last night to be alive? Was he trembling with fear inside those prison walls and locked doors? Not at all! He trusted Jesus to take care of him. If he had to die for Jesus' sake, he was willing to do it. So he went to sleep.

Suddenly Peter was awakened by a slap on his side. He opened his eyes. There was a bright light in the prison! And—could it be true?—there was an angel! "Get up, quickly!" the angel said. *Rattle, rattle!* Peter's chains fell off. "Put on your belt and your sandals," the angel continued. "Wrap your robe around you and follow me."

Peter thought he was dreaming, but he obeyed. In spite of the light and all the noise, the guards didn't stir. They were sound asleep. As Peter and the angel came to the cell door, it opened, and they passed through. They walked through the first and second cell blocks, and the other two guards didn't see them, either. On they went, out into the night. Then they arrived at the last barrier: the huge iron gate. It swung open by itself.

When they reached the city streets, the angel left Peter. "Why, I'm not dreaming," he said. "This is real. I'm free! I'll go and tell the good news to the praying Christians that God has delivered me."

This Is for You

Peter was in a place where there seemed to be no way out. But God had more work for Peter to do in preaching the gospel. So he had an escape plan for him at just the right time.

Do we face difficulties that seem to have no way out? If we don't now, we will someday. Everyone does. They are like prison walls and locked iron gates. What can we do? We can pray and ask others to pray for us. Like Peter who slept in the prison, we can trust God and wait patiently for the answer.

At first, God may show us only one step to take. We should go that far. Then we should keep praying and following him. He holds the keys to all doors—even to the locked iron gate. When we come to that big difficulty that we dreaded, it will have vanished.

Match-Up:
A Cry for God's Help

Like Peter, David was in a jam and needed God. He was hiding in a cave from Saul, who wanted to kill him. He felt he had no way out and that no one cared. Read Psalm 142 about his experience and his prayer. It can be your prayer when you see no way out of your difficulties. Match the sentences below to their proper endings.

1. When David was in great need, he called on
    no one.

2. He told the Lord about his
    refuge.

3. In his path, enemies had set a
    prison.

4. Who cared what happened to him? He said there was
    troubles.

5. He said that the Lord was his
    snare (trap).

6. He asked God to rescue him from his persecutors, for they were too
    the Lord.

7. He wanted God to bring him out of his
    strong.

God did bring David out of his cave and rescued him from his enemies. He made David king of Israel, and many psalms give David's praise and thanks to God for his goodness to him. When we feel down, we can read these psalms to help us see that God can rescue us.

275

Riding on the Wings of an Eagle

Introduction

"Like an eagle that stirs up its nest and hovers over its young, that spreads its wings to catch them and carries them on its pinions. The Lord alone led him."

(Deuteronomy 32:11-12)

HAVE you ever seen a baby learning to walk? A mother holds her little girl's hands and walks along with her. The baby walks, too, on wobbly legs. After a while, the mother lets go, and the baby walks a few steps alone. Then *kerplop!* She sits down flat. Surprised, the baby begins to cry. Mother gently picks her up and walks with her again. They do this over and over, until at last the little girl can walk alone. Was the mother cruel to let the baby fall and maybe get hurt a little bit? No. She was teaching her a valuable lesson.

Moses said that God taught the baby nation of Israel some lessons like a mother eagle teaching her eaglets to fly.

The Facts, Please!

1. An eagle is a bird of prey—a flesh eater. It is one of the largest birds and is very strong. Different species of eagles vary from each other in size, looks, and habits. But all eagles have large, strong bills and powerful claws (talons). All four claws of each foot are sharp and curved. An eagle's feet are well suited for grabbing hold of a small animal and carrying it high into the sky. His bill enables him to tear the flesh of his prey when it is too big to swallow whole.

2. An eagle has very keen eyesight, enabling her to see her prey from hundreds of feet in the air. She swoops down from the sky and seizes and kills the prey. Then she carries it back to her nest, tears it apart, and shares it with her eaglets.

3. An eagle's nest is called an eyrie. These large nests are built high and inaccessible, like in the rocks of a high mountain or on top of a tall tree.

4. When it is time for the eaglets to learn to fly, the mother stirs up the nest, disturbing her little birds into leaving it. She hovers over them as they begin to fall through the air. Then she swoops down under them, bears them up on her outstretched wings, and carries them back to safety. After a few such lessons, the little eaglets learn to copy her wing movements

in the air. They learn what flying is, and soon they can soar through the sky on their own wings.

Bible Story: God Teaches and Cares for Israel
(Deuteronomy 8:1-20)

When the children of Israel left Egypt, they were a new nation. They had many lessons to learn because they didn't know much about God or his laws. As they wandered in the wilderness for 40 years, God taught them and cared for them.

When their leader, Moses, was about to die, there was a new generation of Israelites. All of the older ones were dead (except Joshua and Caleb), so Moses told the younger ones about God's care for their fathers in the wilderness. He told them the laws that God had given. He said that God had been like a mother eagle, teaching her babies to fly.

There was no food in the wilderness. God allowed them to hunger for food, and then he gave them manna to eat. Six days a week for all those years it appeared on the ground. On the sixth day there was enough manna for the seventh day, too. They learned that God and his word are more important than bread.

"We're tired of eating manna," the people complained to God. So he sent fiery serpents that bit them. Then he told them to look at the serpent of brass that Moses set up and they would be healed. They learned that God punishes sin but will forgive and restore them if they will believe him to do it.

When there was no water to drink, God told Moses to

strike a rock. When he did, out came water enough for millions of people. They found out that God could supply all their needs.

God led them through the wilderness by a pillar of cloud by day and a pillar of fire by night. They learned to follow his leadership and to let him take care of them. For 40 years their clothes didn't wear out, and their feet didn't blister or swell as they walked on the burning hot sands.

"Remember these lessons God taught your fathers," Moses told the young people. "Obey him, and he will teach you and care for you, just as an eagle does with her eaglets."

This Is for You

The mother eagle can't let her babies stay in the nest forever. They must learn to fly and take care of themselves. She stirs them out of the nest to teach them the lessons they need to learn. While we are young God helps us learn how to be responsible adults someday. He teaches us to depend on him to take care of us and see us through each situation.

Maybe we have to move from our hometown to live in a strange, new place. We have to get used to a new house and a new school. We are strangers and feel lost and lonesome. God will help us learn to handle the new circumstances, and he'll be there to cheer and comfort us. Perhaps our parents are getting a divorce, or a loved one dies. Maybe our best friend moves away. Jesus understands what we are going though. Right now, every day, we can let him train us to be the best people we can be. We can always count on his support.

Find a Letter and Unscramble Letters:
God's Care for Israel

To finish the sentence below, print the missing letter in each word. Write these letters on the blank line beneath the puzzle. Unscramble them and spell the missing word in the sentence.

__ H O S T

T O A S __

__ H A D E

B R __ A K

T E L __

P A G __

P __ I D

_____

Moses said that God cared for Israel like an eagle caring

for her _____.

Fox Holes and Bird Nests

Introduction

"You know how full of love and kindness our Lord Jesus was: though he was so very rich, yet to help you he became so very poor, so that by being poor he could make you rich."

(2 Corinthians 8:9, TLB)

HAVE you ever walked down a city street and passed by a person who is homeless? If not, you surely have seen pictures of homeless people on TV. Have you ever tried to imagine what it must be like to be homeless? Where would you sleep? How would you keep warm when it's cold or keep dry when it's rainy? How would you keep clean? How would you get food? These problems and many others face homeless people every day.

Did you know that Jesus was homeless? He said, "Foxes have holes and birds of the air have nests, but the Son of Man has no place to lay his head" (Luke 9:58).

The Facts, Please!

1. Fox holes are burrows, or holes in the ground, where foxes live. Foxes were common in the Holy Land in Bible times. They are wild, flesh-eating members of the dog family. Sometimes the foxes dig burrows themselves, and other times they use holes that have been abandoned by other animals. They don't sleep through the winter in their holes, as some ground-dwellers do.

2. Bird nests are structures made or places chosen by birds to lay their eggs and shelter their young. When the little birds leave the nest, the parents usually do, too. Then they live in many different places, depending on the kind of bird.

   Some nests are simple, and others are very elaborate. Shore birds may build nests of a few pebbles or bits of grass. There are birds that build basket-shaped nests on the ground among grasses and weeds or on the fork of a tree's branch. Some birds build little roofs over their nests or entranceway porches. Others find natural holes in trees, cliffs, or in the ground for their homes. Burrowing owls dig large burrows in the ground where they live. Eagles return to the same nests year after year. They repair a nest by adding branches until eventually the nest is a huge structure.

3. Foxes and birds did not discover the best way to build their homes over many years of trying, as evolution teaches. From the very first, God gave them the instinct and intelligence to do this for the protection of themselves and their young.

Bible Story: Jesus' Earthly Home
(John 1:1-14, 17:5; 2 Corinthians 8:9; Philippians 2:6-9)

Long ago, God the Son lived in heaven with the Father and the Holy Spirit. He had always lived there from the beginning of time. In heaven everything is gloriously beautiful and perfect. It has gold, pearls, jewels, and other riches we can only imagine.

One day God the Son left all those riches behind to come to earth. Why? Because all people have sinned. He came to take our place and get punished for our sins so that one day we might go to heaven and enjoy its riches forever. He could not die in the form of God, so he took on the form of man. He was still God, but he left behind his kingly crown and the glory of his majesty.

The Bible says that Jesus became poor so that we might become rich. How poor was he? He was born in a stable and laid in a manger. He was raised in a poor carpenter's home. When he began his ministry, he had no home of his own. As he traveled from place to place, he slept by the seaside, in the mountains, or wherever he could. Sometimes he stayed in the homes of friends, like Mary and Martha. Even the foxes and the birds had homes, but Jesus had no home in which to lay his head.

When Jesus died for our sins, he was nailed to a cross—an awful place where the worst criminals were put to death. There he became the poorest of all. Because our sins were put on him, his heavenly Father had to turn his back on him, for God is too holy to look on sin.

Jesus didn't have a home, even in death. He was laid in a borrowed tomb. But he is God! He came alive again in his glorified body and went back to heaven—never to be poor or homeless again.

This Is for You

Jesus became poor to make us rich when we trust him to save us. How rich are we then? First of all, our sins are gone! We know we'll never suffer in hell.

Right now, in this life, God gives us joy inside, even in troubles and sorrows. We can have peace when things around us aren't peaceful. God will answer our prayers and meet our needs. The Holy Spirit lives inside us to help, guide, and comfort us. We have the Bible to guide our footsteps and to show us how God wants us to live. We will never spend all the riches God has available to us in this life.

In a future day, we will be rich beyond our wildest imagination when we get to heaven. Everything will be beautiful and perfect. There will be no more sorrow or troubles.

Jesus was poor and homeless to give us riches now and forever and a mansion to live in someday. Would you like to thank him for that right now?

Word Search:
When Jesus Became Poor

Circle these words in the puzzle. All of them are found in the Bible story. You can go across, down, and diagonally.

birds	head	manger
carpenter	heaven	nests
cross	holes	poor
death	holy	rich
foxes	home	stable
God (2 times)	man	tomb

```
C R O S S S I N S
A D E A T H O L Y
R F Z M A N G E R
P O O R B G O D N
E Z Z X L I A G E
N H O M E E R O S
T O M B H S Z D T
E M A N H O L E S
R I C H E A V E N
```

The Mighty, Majestic Lion

Introduction

"Be careful—watch out for attacks from Satan, your great enemy. He prowls around like a hungry, roaring lion, looking for some victim to tear apart. Stand firm when he attacks. Trust the Lord."

(1 Peter 5:8-9, TLB)

A huge lion strutted around in the jungle, looking proud. He met first a tiger, then a bear, and then a leopard. Each time he grabbed hold of the animal and asked, "Who is the king of the beasts?"

Each of the animals answered, "You are, O mighty lion."

Then the lion asked an elephant, "Who is the king of the beasts?" The elephant lifted the lion right off the ground with his trunk and slammed him against a tree. The bruised, bleeding lion got up feebly and said, "Well, you don't have to get so rough just because you don't know the answer!"

The Facts, Please!

1. The lion is often called the "king of beasts." The male lion's mane, his powerful frame, and his large head give him a stately, regal appearance. A full-grown male measures nearly 4 feet high and is 9 or 10 feet long, from nose to tip of tail. Male lions weigh about 400 to 500 pounds. The more slender lioness looks like a male without its mane.

2. A lion's tail ends in a tuft, in the center of which is a sort of claw, known as its "thorn." The powerful fore-legs and large feet with sharp, horny claws are power-ful weapons.

3. A lion doesn't spend most of his time hunting his prey. He sleeps up to 20 hours a day, either in his den or beneath a shade tree. He hunts at night under the cover of darkness. Of course, he doesn't roar then! He creeps silently close to his prey, staying downwind of his prey to keep the animal from getting his scent.

4. A lion doesn't look for the biggest animal to kill. He attacks old, young, or weak animals because they are easier to hunt down. When he is near his victim, he rushes toward it with great speed and leaps on it. He kills small prey with a single swat of his paw, or he breaks the neck of a larger animal.

5. Lions were plentiful in Palestine in Bible times. The

Bible has many stories of lions, and verses where they are mentioned. Lions don't often attack and kill men, but they have done so. The following four stories are about lions and men.

Bible Story: Lion Attack!
(Judges 14:5-7; 1 Samuel 17:34-37; 2 Samuel 23:20; Daniel 6:16-23)

Story One: Manoah and his wife had no children. One day an angel appeared to her. "You shall have a son," he said. "You must give him to God from his birth. As a sign of this, he shall not cut his hair. Before he is born, you must not drink wine or strong drink or eat forbidden meat." When the baby was born, Manoah and his wife named him Samson. He grew to be the strongest man that the Bible tells us about.

One day, when Samson was about 20 years old, he was walking through a vineyard. Suddenly a young lion leaped out with a roar and attacked him. Samson had no weapon, but the Spirit of the Lord came on him, and he tore the fierce lion's jaws apart as if it had been a goat.

Story Two: When David was caring for his father's sheep one day, a lion sneaked up and took a lamb from his flock. David chased the lion, struck it, and seized the lamb from its mouth. When the lion turned to attack David, he grabbed it by its mane, struck it, and killed it. "God delivered me from the paw of the lion," David said.

Story Three: One snowy day a lion fell into a pit—perhaps a trap that people had set to catch him. Benaiah jumped into the slippery pit and killed the lion all by himself. King David said Benaiah was one of his bravest men.

Story Four: Daniel was thrown into a den of hungry lions just because he prayed to God. He had no way of escape. Surely the lions would attack him and eat him! But they didn't because God sent his angel to shut the lions' mouths. Daniel came out of the lions' den safe and sound.

This Is for You

God protected all of these Bible men in their encounters with lions. He helped three of the men kill the lions. He shut the lions' mouths for Daniel.

We will probably never be attacked by a real lion. But the Bible says that the devil goes about like a roaring lion, trying to find those whom he can attack. He can't kill us, but he can tempt us to sin. We need God's help to resist him.

God warns us to watch out for him. Like a lion who attacks old or weak animals, Satan comes after us especially when we are tired or weak in our body or troubled in our mind. He sees when we fail to read the Bible, pray, and go to church. He knows this means we are drifting away from God. At times like that, he sneaks up on us and snares us into sin.

Let's keep the lines open between us and God. Then when Satan attacks, we can stand firm against him, depending on God's help. He can take care of lions, especially that old lion, the devil.

Write Your Own Answer:
What You Can Do When Satan Attacks You

A lion sneaks up and pounces on his prey when it is not watching carefully. Satan can come up on you with his temptations just like that. Jesus said, "Watch and pray so that you will not fall into temptation" (Mark 14:38). Write on the lines below what you can do to resist temptation in the situations given.

1. You are invited to go to a place where you know you are easily tempted to sin. What do you think you should do? _____

_____

2. There is someone at home or school who is always doing something to make you angry and upset. What can you do to stay calm and not lose your temper?

_____

_____

3. A big test is coming up at school, and the smartest kid in class sits next to you. What can you do to keep from being tempted to look at his paper and copy his answers? _____

_____

4. You are sometimes tempted to lie to your parents to keep from getting punished. What can you do to avoid that temptation? _____

_____

Whips and Scourges

Introduction

"But he was wounded and bruised for our sins. He was beaten that we might have peace; he was lashed—and we were healed!"

(Isaiah 53:5, TLB)

Long ago, in a little one-room mountain school, a new teacher arrived. He knew that the boys in the school were very rough and disobedient, so he had the children help him make up 10 rules they must obey. The worst trouble-maker, Tom, said, "If someone breaks a rule, I think he oughta get a lickin' on his back 10 times with his coat off."

One day Tom's lunch was stolen. The thief was found—a skinny little boy named Jim. The teacher brought him to the front of the room and told him to take off his coat. "Please don't make me take it off," Jim pleaded.

"He's gotta do it!" yelled out Tom, so Jim pulled off his coat. Underneath, he had on no shirt.

"Father died, and we're real poor. I only have one shirt, and Mother is washing it today," Jim said. The teacher was wondering how he could whip that bare, skinny back when Tom walked up.

"I'll take his whipping," Tom said. Little Jim watched as Tom took off his coat and stood still to get 10 lashes.

"Tom, I took your lunch 'cause I was so hungry," Jim said. "Please forgive me. Thank you for taking my lickin'. I'll love you until I die!"

The Facts, Please!

1. In Bible times, whips and scourges were used to flog animals and to punish people. They were usually made of a rod, with a lash on one end.

2. The whip that Jesus used two different times to cleanse the temple was made of small cords of rope.

3. The scourge that the Roman soldiers used to whip Jesus had three leather thongs which were weighted with sharp pieces of lead or bone. They could tear the flesh off both the back and the breast of the person being scourged.

4. The Roman method of scourging was to strip a person to the waist and tie him in a bending position to a pillar. By Jewish law, the number of lashes must be

no more than 40. Usually 39 lashes were given to be sure the scourgers didn't miscount and give more than 40.

Bible Story: Jesus and the Whips
(John 2:13-17; 19:1-7)

It was time for the Passover celebration in Jerusalem. Jesus, along with thousands of other people, went to the temple. As he came into the Court of the Gentiles, Jesus heard oxen lowing, sheep bleating, and doves cooing. Animals and men crowded together, and money changers sat behind their tables.

The Court of the Gentiles, which was supposed to be a place of worship, was like a crowded marketplace. The money changers were charging people a big fee to exchange their foreign money for coins to pay the temple tax. Merchants sold the animals to people who needed them for sacrifices. Their price was far above what the animals were worth.

Jesus found some small ropes and bound them together like a whip. He chased out the merchants and money changers. He drove out the animals and overturned the money tables, scattering the coins all over the floor. "Get out!" he said. "Don't make my Father's house a marketplace!"

A little over three years later, Jesus himself was whipped. Had he done something bad, as those merchants and money changers had? Did he deserve a scourging? Oh no! It was part of the punishment he took for our sins.

Roman soldiers stripped Jesus to the waist and tied his hands to a post, bending his back down. They took the scourge, with bits of sharp lead in it, and beat him again and again—39 lashes in all. They thought Jesus was helpless and could not save himself from all that pain. But they were wrong. Earlier, in the garden, Jesus told his captors, "Don't you know that I could ask my Father for thousands of angels to rescue me, and he would send them?"

He could have called for angels' help, but he didn't. He could have destroyed the soldiers with one word. But he said nothing. After the terrible beating and much more cruelty, Jesus let the wicked men crucify him. He took the punishment gladly because he loves us all so much.

This Is for You

Let's imagine ourselves present at Jesus' trial and crucifixion. We see him as the cruel men scourge him, place a crown of thorns on his head, spit in his face, and nail him to a cross. He is suffering through all this to take the punishment for our sin.

How can we thank Jesus for what he did for us? First, we can receive his free gift of salvation, asking him to forgive our sins and receiving him as our Savior and Lord. Then, we should love him with all our heart. If we do, he will come first in our life. We will do our best to obey him and serve him.

This would be a good time to say to Jesus, as Jim did to Tom, "Please forgive me. Thank you for taking my lickin'. I'll love you until I die!"

Cross Out Letters:
Why Jesus Came and Why He Died

In the cross below, black out the letters B, G, K, P, Q, X, Y, Z. Print the remaining letters on the lines, in order from the top to the bottom, going from left to right.

```
            B C H Q
            R G I S
            T X Z J
            K E S P
    U S C A M E B I N T O Y
    T H E K W O R L D Z T Z
    O G K S A B G V E S I N
    N X Y Z E Z R S Y Y Z Q
            G K B C
            B G H R
            P Q X I
            S T Z D
            Z I Y E
            D F Q O
            B G R O
            X U R S
            I K N S
```

"_____

_____" (1 Timothy 1:15).

"_____

_____" (1 Corinthians 15:3).

ANSWERS

DEVOTION 1 (p. 4)

1. God's tiny dive-bombers are <u>HORNETS</u>.
2. Hornets belong to the family of insects called <u>WASPS</u>.
3. Hornets are called "social wasps" because they live in <u>COLONIES</u>.
4. Hornets make their paper nests from old <u>WOOD</u> and tough <u>PLANT</u> <u>FIBERS</u>.
5. A hornet's stinger is located in the rear tip of the <u>ABDOMEN</u>.
6. The land God gave the Israelites is called <u>CANAAN</u>.
7. God told the Israelites to drive out or destroy the people who were living in Canaan because they were <u>WICKED</u> and <u>WORSHIPED</u> <u>IDOLS</u>.
8. To help drive out Israel's enemies, the Lord sent <u>HORNETS</u>.
9. A Christian's enemy is <u>SATAN</u>.
10. Satan's fiery darts are his <u>TEMPTATIONS</u>.
11. Two weapons you can use against Satan are the <u>BIBLE</u> and <u>PRAYER</u>.
12. The one who will give you the most help in your fight against Satan is <u>GOD</u>.

DEVOTION 2 (p. 10)

It has happened at last! <u>JESUS</u> has left <u>HEAVEN</u> and is now in the <u>AIR</u> above the <u>EARTH</u>. Gabriel's voice was heard, and the <u>TRUMP</u> of God sounded. The bodies of <u>DEAD</u>

believers that had been <u>DUST</u> are now <u>ALIVE</u>. Living believers have their new <u>BODIES</u>. They are all <u>MEETING</u> the <u>LORD</u> in the air. Soon they will pass through the <u>PEARLY</u> gates to spend <u>ETERNITY</u> here. Welcome, <u>CHILDREN</u> of God! Welcome to the heavenly <u>CITY</u>!

DEVOTION 3 (p. 16)

DEVOTION 4 (p. 22)

1. The little girl asked God for some <u>RED</u> <u>SHOES</u>, and he answered her <u>PRAYER</u>.

2. In ancient days, tools were made from hard <u>STONE</u> and later from <u>BRONZE</u>. Finally, they were made from <u>IRON</u>.

3. The prophet who was the head teacher at the school of the <u>PROPHETS</u> was <u>ELISHA</u>.

4. There were so many students living at the school, that they needed more <u>ROOM</u>.

5. They went to the <u>JORDAN</u> River to cut down trees and build a bigger place to live.

6. One young man's <u>AXHEAD</u> fell into the <u>WATER</u>.

7. He was worried because he had <u>BORROWED</u> the ax.

8. Elisha threw a <u>STICK</u> in the water, and the axhead <u>FLOATED</u>.

9. <u>GOD</u> worked a miracle by suspending the law of gravitation.

Devotion 5 (p. 29)

1. Psalm 19:7: The law of the Lord is——perfect

2. Psalm 12:6: The words of the Lord are like purified (refined)——silver

3. Psalm 119:127: The psalmist said he loved God's commandments more than pure——gold

4. Deuteronomy 11:27: If we obey God's commandments, we will have a——blessing

5. 2 Timothy 3:16: How much Scripture is inspired of God (God-breathed)?——all

6. Psalm 119:11: We should hide God's Word in our heart that we might not——sin

7. 1 Peter 1:25: The Word of the Lord lasts——forever

8. Psalm 33:4: The Word of the Lord is——right

9. John 20:31: The Bible was written that we might believe that Jesus is the Christ, the Son of God, and that by believing we might have——life

Devotion 6 (p. 35)

1. The strange little leather boxes were called <u>PHYLACTERIES</u>.

2. These were worn on the arm and on the <u>FOREHEAD</u>.

3. A very important religious group of Jews was the <u>PHARISEES</u>.

4. Many Pharisees seemed good but they didn't love <u>GOD</u>.

5. One who loved God and came to see Jesus one night was named <u>NICODEMUS</u>.

6. The difference between the good and the bad Pharisees was the condition of their <u>HEARTS</u>.

   Scrambled letters:

   First word: Y C I R P H O E T

   Second word: C I R H I N S A T

1. A professor of Jesus who doesn't possess him is a <u>HYPOCRITE</u>.

2. A possessor of Jesus is a <u>CHRISTIAN</u>.

DEVOTION 7 (p. 41)

```
H-W  O-N  E-L-O-R
O-I  S   T-H  D-I  D
O-S  I  W  ?  E  S-S
N-T  O-H  E  ?  W-H
E-H  D-S  D  H-T  O
L-O-R  S-I  E  N  I
D-I-S  R-O-L  O-S
E  ?  S-D
```

DEVOTION 8 (p. 47)

Cleansing from sin——1 John 1:9——Confess sins

Long life——Ephesians 6:2-3——Honor your parents

Gifts from God——Luke 6:38——Give to God

Wisdom——James 1:5-6——Ask and believe God

Answers to prayer——1 John 3:22——Obey and please God

Blessings from God——Psalm 24:4-5——Have clean hands and a pure heart

Peace——Psalm 119:165——Love God's laws

DEVOTION 9 (p. 53)

ACROSS

4. To "take the yoke of" means to follow a certain <u>TEACHER</u>.

5. <u>OXEN</u> were commonly used for pulling a plow.

10. A yoke was usually made from <u>WOOD</u>.

11. A man's coat worn over his other clothes was called a <u>MANTLE</u>.

12. Elisha lived near the <u>JORDAN</u> River.

DOWN

1. Only seven thousand Israelites did not worship the false god BAAL.

2. A prophet's mantle was made of SHEEPSKIN.

3. Elijah was a great PROPHET.

6. God chose ELISHA to be the prophet after Elijah.

7. Elisha was the son of a rich FARMER.

8. A harness that connected a pair of animals for work was called a YOKE.

9. ELIJAH put his mantle on Elisha's shoulders.

```
      B
      A   S   P
  T E A C H E R
      L   E   O X E N
    F     E   P   L
    A     P   H   I         Y
E   R     S   E   S     W O O D
L   M     K   T   H           K
I   E     I       M A N T L E
J O R D A N
A
H
```

DEVOTION 10 (p. 59)

1. Workers with clay are called POTTERS.

2. They can only work with a special kind of CLAY.

3. Pottery clay must be able to retain its SHAPE.

4. It must harden under a high TEMPERATURE.

5. Pottery is molded on a potter's WHEEL.

6. The man God sent to the potter's house was <u>JEREMIAH</u>.

7. The potter had a marred pot that he <u>SMASHED</u> and <u>MOLDED</u>.

God is our <u>POTTER</u>.

We are his <u>CLAY</u>.

He wants us to <u>YIELD</u> ourselves to him.

Devotion 11 (p. 65)

"Now is the accepted time; now is the day of salvation" (2 Corinthians 6:2, KJV).

When is the most important time to ask Jesus to save you? Now.

Devotion 12 (p. 71)

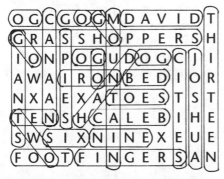

Devotion 13 (p. 77)

<u>JESUS</u> came down from <u>HEAVEN</u> to <u>EARTH</u> to be <u>PUNISHED</u> by dying on the <u>CROSS</u> for <u>OUR SINS</u>. He was laid in a <u>TOMB</u>. Because he is <u>GOD</u>, he <u>AROSE</u> from the dead and went back <u>UP</u> to heaven and wore his <u>CROWN</u> as King. What a <u>SAVIOR</u> Jesus is!

Devotion 14 (p. 83)

Dear Simon,

It is a lovely <u>SPRING</u> day here in <u>JERUSALEM</u>. Soon there will be a <u>FULL</u> <u>MOON</u> and we will celebrate <u>PASSOVER</u>. Father has asked me to write and invite you and your family to visit us during all the days of the <u>FEAST</u> of <u>UNLEAVENED</u> <u>BREAD</u>. We have already picked out a special <u>LAMB</u> to be <u>SACRIFICED</u> and <u>ROASTED</u> for our <u>SUPPER</u>. We will have unleavened <u>BREAD</u>, bitter <u>HERBS</u>, and charoseth <u>SAUCE</u>. How happy it will make all of us if you can come!

Your cousin,
Jacob

Devotion 15 (p. 88)

Verse 2: <u>ANGELS</u>

Verse 3: <u>SUN</u>, <u>MOON</u>, <u>STARS</u>

Verse 4: <u>HEAVENS</u> (<u>SKIES</u>—TLB)

Verse 9: <u>MOUNTAINS</u>, <u>HILLS</u>, <u>FRUIT</u> <u>TREES</u>, <u>CEDARS</u>

Verse 11: <u>KINGS</u>

Verse 12: <u>YOUNG</u> <u>MEN</u>, <u>MAIDENS</u>, <u>OLD</u> <u>MEN</u>, <u>CHILDREN</u>

Devotion 16 (p. 95)

1. Every year the Israelites had a special camping trip to celebrate the——Feast of Tabernacles.

2. It was held in the——fall.

3. It was a time of thanksgiving for——the harvest.

4. Everyone lived in shelters (booths) for——seven days.

5. This reminded them that for 40 years the Israelites lived in the desert in——tents.

6. The shelters were made of four poles and a framework into which were woven——tree limbs and leaves.

7. In Jerusalem the priests led a procession to get water from——the Pool of Siloam.

8. For 40 years in the desert God provided the hungry and thirsty people with——food and water.

9. In all those years the people did not need new——clothes and shoes.

Devotion 17 (p. 101)

T H E Y   B U I L T   F I N E   H O M E S   B U T   D I D   N O T

B U I L D   G O D' S   H O U S E.

T H E Y   B E G A N   T O   B U I L D   G O D' S   H O U S E.

Devotion 18 (p. 107)

1. Nebuchadnezzar was the <u>KING</u> of Babylon who fought against God's people, the <u>JEWS</u>, and their king, Zedekiah.

2. Jeremiah was a <u>PROPHET</u> who <u>TOLD</u> God's message to the Jews.

3. Jeremiah said, "<u>GOD</u> wants you to surrender to Nebuchadnezzar."

4. The Jews called him a <u>TRAITOR</u> and put him in a <u>CISTERN</u> with deep <u>MUD</u> in the bottom.

5. Zedekiah let Ebed-Melech rescue Jeremiah. Ebed-Melech gave Jeremiah old <u>RAGS</u> for under his <u>ARMPITS</u> and pulled him up with <u>ROPES</u>.

6. Nebuchadnezzar and his <u>ARMIES</u> captured Jerusalem and burned it down. Zedekiah and most Jews were taken to Babylon.

7. God took care of Jeremiah, because he was <u>TRUE</u> and faithful to God.

Devotion 19 (p. 113)

Talking back to parents——Ephesians 6:2

Stealing or cheating——Exodus 20:15

Complaining about going to church——Psalm 122:1

Not praying when tempted to sin——Matthew 26:41

Disobeying parents——Ephesians 6:1

Cursing——Exodus 20:7

Not reading and studying the Bible——2 Timothy 2:15

Loving to do worldly things——1 John 2:15

Lying——Ephesians 4:25

Devotion 20 (p. 119)

In Bible days, there were no <u>SATELLITES</u> in the sky to spy out enemy troop movements. There were no warning systems, using <u>TELEVISIONS</u> or telephones to alert the public of danger. But they did have a way to warn people when danger approached. They had <u>WATCHMEN</u> who stayed in <u>WATCHTOWERS</u> as lookouts. If an enemy or any other kind of trouble approached, they would blow an <u>ALARM</u> with a <u>TRUMPET</u>.

If a watchman sounded an alarm and the people did not seek safety and then <u>DIED</u>, it was their own <u>FAULT</u>. If a watchman saw danger and didn't sound an alarm, he was held <u>RESPONSIBLE</u> if people died.

All Christians are to be God's <u>WATCHMEN</u>, warning sinners that they will stand before God on <u>JUDGMENT DAY</u> and spend eternity in <u>HELL</u> if they don't repent and believe in <u>JESUS</u> as <u>SAVIOR</u>. What kind of watchman are <u>YOU</u>?

Devotion 21 (p. 125)

Saul <u>A S K E D</u> God for help, but got no answer.

He <u>I N Q U I R E D</u> of a medium, asking her

to <u>B R I N G</u> up Samuel from the dead.

<u>G O D</u> brought up Samuel's spirit.

Seeing the <u>S P I R I T</u>, the medium

screamed. Saul <u>A S K E D</u> Samuel for help.

<u>S A M U E L</u> said that the

<u>I S R A E L I T E S</u> would be defeated, and Saul

and his sons would die, and it was so!

Devotion 22 (p. 131)

1. BELSHAZZAR KNEW ABOUT GOD.

2. HE DID NOT HONOR GOD.

3. HE DRANK FROM CUPS OUT OF GOD'S TEMPLE.

4. HE PRAISED FALSE MAN-MADE GODS.

Devotion 23 (p. 137)

Man is a Supreme Being; put faith and trust in man.——God is the Supreme Being; believe in him. (Isaiah 45:21-22)

Man is an animal, having only a soul and body.——God made man in his image—body, soul, and spirit. (Genesis 1:27; 1 Thessalonians 5:23)

There is no life after death.——There is life after death. (1 Corinthians 15:52)

The earth and people came into being by evolution.——God created the heavens and the earth. (Genesis 1:1)

There is no such thing as sin.——All people have sinned. (Romans 3:23)

There is no devil.——There is a devil (Satan). (1 Peter 5:8)

Devotion 24 (p. 143)

Sentence 1: RICHES

Sentence 2: JESUS

Devotion 25 (p. 148)

There is a <u>WORM</u> called the <u>TOLA</u> that is <u>CRUSHED</u>

      (1 down)   (4 across)   (6 down)

so that its <u>BLOOD</u> can be made into a <u>CRIMSON</u>
(5 across)   (6 across)

<u>DYE</u>. Psalm 22:6 says that Jesus felt like a worm, not a
(7 across)

<u>MAN</u>, when he <u>DIED</u> for our <u>SINS</u>. He was
(8 down)   (13 across)   (14 across)

mocked and <u>LAUGHED</u> at, even though he is the King of
(2 across)

<u>GLORY</u>. The tola worm gave its blood to provide crimson
(3 down)

robes. Jesus died to give us <u>ROBES</u> of <u>SALVATION</u>
(9 down)   (10 across)

that are as white as <u>SNOW</u>. Isn't his <u>LOVE</u> wonderful?
(12 down)   (11 down)

		W			L	A	U	G	H	E	D
	T	O	L	A				L			
		R			B	L	O	O	D		
C	R	I	M	S	O	N		R			
R					D	Y	E				
U			M		R						
S	A	L	V	A	T	I	O	N			
H		O		N		B					
E		V			E		S				
D	I	E	D		S	I	N	S			
					O						
					W						

Devotion 27 (p. 161)

stern——the back of a ship

prow (bow)——the front of a ship

mainsail——the large, principal sail

foresail——a small, auxiliary sail

hull——the frame of a ship

mast——tall spar, rising vertically from a ship's deck

rudders——movable paddles for steering a ship

anchor——a weight to keep a ship from drifting

"helps" (KJV)——ropes or chains tied around a ship's hull in a storm

cargo vessel——a ship that carries freight

navigation——plotting a ship's course

Devotion 29 (p. 173)

PSALM 119:11: Hide (store) God's <u>WORD</u> in your <u>HEART</u> so you won't <u>SIN</u>.

LUKE 22:40: <u>PRAY</u> that you won't fall into temptation.

PROVERBS 1:8: <u>LISTEN</u> to the teachings of your <u>FATHER</u> and <u>MOTHER</u>.

PROVERBS 4:14-15: Don't follow in the ways of the <u>WICKED</u>.

EPHESIANS 6:11: Put on the full <u>ARMOR</u> of God, so you can stand against the tricks of the <u>DEVIL</u>.

EPHESIANS 6:16. Use the shield of <u>FAITH</u>.

Devotion 30 (p. 179)

To God, you are somebody S P E C I A L.

God can use you if you will trust him and not be A F R A I D.

Devotion 31 (p. 185)

First Trumpet Call: "Believe on the Lord Jesus Christ, and thou shalt be saved" (Acts 16:31).

Second Trumpet Call: "Thou therefore endure hardness, as a good soldier of Jesus Christ" (2 Timothy 2:3).

Third Trumpet Call: "And, behold, I come quickly; and my reward is with me" (Revelation 22:12).

Devotion 32 (p. 191)

Fig leaves——Aprons made by Adam and Eve to try to cover themselves

Furs——Coats made by God for Adam and Eve to wear

Filthy rags——Clothing worn by people who trust in their good deeds for their salvation, not in Jesus

Garment of salvation——Spiritual clothing given to anyone who repents of sin and trusts Christ as Savior

Robe of righteousness——Another name for the garment of salvation—made, not of our own goodness, but of Christ's

Fine linen, clean and white——Robes worn at the wedding feast in heaven by the bride of Christ

Devotion 34 (p. 203)

HAROAPH	PHARAOH
SEMOS	MOSES
RANOA	AARON
ODG	GOD
GSORF	FROGS
NEVO	OVEN
DEB	BED
GUDOH	DOUGH
MASSTRE	STREAMS
VERISR	RIVERS
TEEF	FEET

God can do everything, because there is NOTHING TOO HARD for him.

Devotion 35 (p. 209)

D-O I S-W C-A E-A I-N-S
B G-F U H-O N-B G-A U-T
E-F-O-R U-R-O-F D-O S-?
I-A E-B S-W-H E-B G-F-I
N G-A N-A-C-O O-D F-O-R
S-T-U-S ? I-F-G B-E S-U
I ?-S-U-T-S A-G B-N W-H
F D-B O-R N-I A-E A-C-O
G-O E-F U-S W C-A E-A-G
N-A H-W R-O H-O N-B I-A
B C-O S-U F D-O I ? N-S
E A-I T-U E-B G-F S-U-T
A-G N-S S-?

Devotion 36 (p. 215)

NEWS FLASH! THE <u>ARK</u> OF <u>GOD</u> IS <u>STOLEN</u>!

A terrific <u>BATTLE</u> happened today near Ebenezer between the <u>ISRAELITE</u> army and the <u>PHILISTINES</u>. To make sure that God would be with them, the Israelites took along the <u>ARK</u> of <u>GOD</u>. A great <u>SHOUT</u> went up from their <u>CAMP</u> when it arrived. But there was no <u>HELP</u> from God. The <u>PHILISTINES</u> fought very hard, and they <u>KILLED</u> <u>THIRTY</u> thousand Israelite <u>FOOT</u>soldiers. Then, worst of all, they <u>STOLE</u> the <u>ARK</u> of <u>GOD</u>. All hope is gone for its <u>RETURN</u> from enemy territory.

Devotion 37 (p. 221)

I would not worship <u>IDOLS</u>
Of metal, wood, or <u>STONE</u>;
But do I worship other <u>THINGS</u>
Instead of God <u>ALONE</u>?

Whatever comes between <u>US</u>,
My wondrous God and <u>ME</u>
A place, a person, or a <u>THING</u>
That can my idol <u>BE</u>.

Dear Jesus, I will choose <u>YOU</u>
To be my Lord and <u>KING</u>.
I want to put you first of <u>ALL</u>
In each and every <u>THING</u>.

Devotion 38 (p. 227)

Those who <u>SAIL</u> on the <u>SEA</u> in <u>SHIPS</u> see the works of the Lord and his <u>WONDERS</u> in the deep. The stormy <u>WINDS</u> lift the <u>WAVES</u> high. Their ships rise up to the <u>HEAVENS</u> and sink down into the <u>DEPTHS</u>. The sailors are at their <u>WITS'</u> end. They <u>CRY</u> to the Lord, and he <u>CALMS</u> the storm. Then they are <u>GLAD</u>, and the Lord brings them safely to their <u>HARBOR</u>. <u>PRAISE</u> the Lord for his wonderful <u>WORKS</u> to <u>YOU</u>!

Devotion 39 (p. 233)

"FOR THE WAGES OF SIN IS DEATH, BUT THE GIFT OF GOD IS ETERNAL LIFE THROUGH JESUS CHRIST OUR LORD."

Devotion 40 (p. 239)

Devotion 41 (p. 245)

The Jews <u>MET</u> together. They <u>BOWED</u> to the ground and
      (6 down)   (2 down)

<u>WORSHIPED</u> God. They <u>LISTENED</u> to the reading
 (7 across)   (8 across)

of God's Book. They <u>WEPT</u> over their sins. They <u>ATE</u> and
        (3 down)   (5 down)

<u>DRANK</u> in a joyful celebration. They <u>GAVE</u> food to the
(9 across)   (4 across)

poor. They <u>REJOICED</u> that they heard and understood
      (1 down)

God's laws.

DEVOTION 42 (p. 251)

DEVOTION 43 (p. 257)

1. FOE
2. FRIENDS
3. FRIENDS
4. FRIENDS
5. FOES

6. FRIEND

7. FRIEND

8. FOE

9. FRIEND

DEVOTION 44 (p. 263)

He was in danger in WATERS, with ROBBERS, from his own PEOPLE and from the Gentiles, in the CITIES, in the DESERT, and in the SEA. He was WEARY and in PAIN from his labors and toils; he watched through nights when he had no SLEEP. He was HUNGRY, THIRSTY, and didn't have enough CLOTHES to keep him warm.

DEVOTION 45 (p. 269)

"Master, we have toiled all the night, and have taken nothing: nevertheless at thy word I will let down the net."

DEVOTION 46 (p. 275)

1. When David was in great need, he called on——the Lord.

2. He told the Lord about his——troubles.

3. In his path, enemies had set a——snare (trap).

4. Who cared what happened to him? He said there was——no one.

5. He said that the Lord was his——refuge.

6. He asked God to rescue him from his persecutors, for they were too——strong.

7. He wanted God to bring him out of his——prison.

DEVOTION 47 (p. 281)

GHOST

TOAST

SHADE

BREAK

TELL

PAGE

PAID

GTSELEA

Moses said that God cared for Israel like an eagle caring for her <u>EAGLETS</u>.

DEVOTION 48 (p. 287)

DEVOTION 50 (p. 299)

"<u>CHRIST JESUS CAME INTO THE WORLD TO SAVE SINNERS</u>" (1 Timothy 1:15).

"<u>CHRIST DIED FOR OUR SINS</u>" (1 Corinthians 15:3).

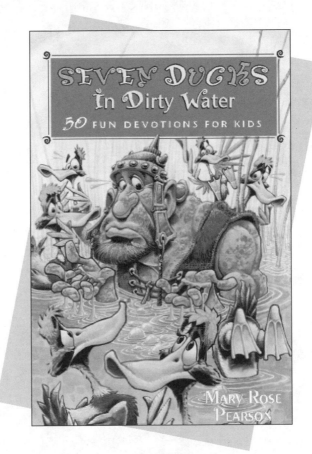